ON THE BUSES

Recollections of a West Bromwich busman

by Harry Rees

ISBN No. 1 872863 08 6

Printed and published by Kithead Ltd,
De Salis Drive, Hampton Lovett, Droitwich Spa, Worcs, WR9 0QE

CONTENTS

FOREWORD

A few years ago I wrote down some recollections of my career on the buses with West Bromwich Corporation Transport and circulated them to a number of friends and acquaintances. Being well received, I was encouraged to embark upon this enlarged version which I think will also form an outline of the Department's history and which I hope may be enjoyed by anyone who reads it.

I would like to record a number of thanks in connection with this little venture. First of all, I am glad to record the encouragement, general help and advice of David Harvey who also undertook the re-typing of my original draft and supplied many of the illustrations. Peter Jaques has also contributed a number of useful items which I have included and I also thank him for making all the necessary arrangements for publication. Alan Mills and Don Phipps have kindly read and commented on my final draft.

The number of pictures has been considerably expanded and I am indebted to all the various photographers who have consented to their work being reproduced. There are one or two photographs taken by people whom I have been unable to trace in order to seek their permission but they were such that I felt that they must be included and I hope that no offence will be taken.

Finally I would like to mention my friend and former colleague Alan Crabb, whose idea it was that my original booklet should be expanded to form the present book.

HARRY REES
May 1995

EARLY DAYS

I was reading an article in a "Black Country Bugle" some years ago when I realised that it was written by one Ernest Crump. It concerned his memories of being employed on the West Bromwich Corporation buses some fifty to sixty years ago and I realized that this was the same person that I first met on Leap Year Day 1928, when I joined the Transport Department as a bus conductor.

The article prompted me to recollect my own career working for West Bromwich Corporation. I would have much preferred to have found employment in the engineering side of the Transport Department but jobs were scarce at the end of the twenties and the prospect of regular employment was not to be missed.

I can remember many of the characters who were working "On The Buses" at that time. Two of the Inspectors, Tommy Jones and Reuben Richards, both wore the traditional breeches and leather leggings which had been the normal clothing but by the late 1920s was becoming something of a rarity. A lot of the bus drivers who were employed at that time come to mind. There were Walter Allen, Ernest Bratt who later became the Mayor's Chauffeur, Bill Callaghan, Harold Fenton, Bill Holyhead, Harry Holland, who was later to become Chief Inspector, Johnny Lester, Alf Morton, Bill Plant, H.Shepperd and Harry Timmins. There were about seven conductresses employed at this early date and I can remember three of them clearly. There was Liza Jukes who later hung up her ticket rack and became Canteen Manageress and Daisy Holyhead and Nellie Timmins, both later transferred to the ticket office. I also recall Conductors Alf Harrison, D. Ready, C. Sheppard and J. Taylor.

The office accommodation was extremely small, consisting of two small rooms which acted as the Manager's office, the typing office, the stores and spares, repository and the ticket office. Anything else which was required to run the operation was also stored there! The administration side consisted of the General Manager, Mr A. Witcomb

Smith, his assistant Mr W. Whitwell and the secretary-cum-typist, Miss Cheshire who occupied the best offices at the garage premises.

At that time the bus operation occupied a garage within the Corporation Highways Department in Hardware Street. There were about eleven buses at that time and of these, about five or six were housed in the garage and the remainder in the yard outside. The maintenance of the buses was carried out under the supervision of the foreman G. Goodwin, with able assistance from mechanics J. Ashby, H. Groves, E.O. Radcliffe, A. Palmer and the cleaner Harry Fitzpatrick.

Buses returning to the garage at Hardware Street at night were filled with petrol in the Highways yard before being parked by the driver. I well remember on Saturday nights that Harry Fitzpatrick's job was to wait for all the bus fleet to return from their late night services. He then had to fill up the buses with petrol from the one pump which was available; this was hand-operated and so the buses could only be filled up a gallon at a time, which was not an attractive job on a winter's night, especially as there was no canopy or forecourt to offer protection from the weather.

In 1929, West Bromwich purchased the Smethwick sections of the Spon Croft and Bromford Lane tram routes run by the Birmingham District Power and Traction Co. Ltd (the part in West Bromwich was already owned by the Corporation) and West Bromwich buses replaced the company trams on Sunday 18 November 1929, only one day after public notice had been given!   Part of the deal to take over the tram routes involved the employment of five of the tramway conductors. The five of them were Horace Armstrong, Albert Cole, Fred Gannon, George Hoey and Jack Perrins.

With the Town Council's policy of slum clearance and the building of new council housing, new bus services and therefore extra buses in the fleet, became necessary. In order to keep pace with the demands being placed on the Department, more drivers and conductors were recruited, so that the number of employees began to grow at a very fast rate.

This expansion and the extra buses for the "Lanes" (as the ex-company tram routes were known) caused some difficulties not least in housing the expanded bus fleet in the limited accommodation available in the Hardware Street premises. To alleviate this problem a new garage was planned, half a mile away; this was the Oak Lane garage opened in 1930. This new garage had all the modern equipment of the period, enabling over sixty buses to be parked and serviced under cover. There were electrically operated petrol pumps, glazed and well-lit inspection pits, day and night stores, tyre and oil stores. There was also an extensive office block, canteen, toilets and washing facilities as well as coach building and painting shops.

To mark the opening of the new garage, the Transport Committee decided to give all its employees a day's outing. This was an extremely generous gesture as transport and lunch were provided free with no loss of pay for the day involved. The trip was run in two halves on two separate days, to Evesham, as of course the bus services still had to operate as normal although only half the staff was present to operate them. This involved additional time being worked by the staff on duty but every individual responded with enthusiasm and so the bus service was maintained. The three buses left for Evesham at 10 a.m. and all concerned had a wonderful day out, the second party going the following week.

The following year the outing was repeated, once again to Evesham and it became an annual event visiting various places over the years. The most adventurous outings were in 1938 and 1939 when the trip was to Blackpool. The traffic staff worked the first part of their duty as usual until 9.30 a.m. and were taken by bus to Dudley Port Station. From there they were taken by train to Blackpool, where seven or eight hours was spent and on the return journey had dinner on the train. Buses met the party at Dudley Port to convey them back to Oak Lane Garage. The cost of the journey and dinner was borne most generously by the Transport Committee.

These trips were, of course, ended by the outbreak of war in 1939 but in the 1950s representation was made to the Committee by the Transport & General Workers Union for the re-establishment of the annual day outing and this was granted. However, owing to the increased number of services then in operation, the trip was arranged to be run on four successive Sundays so that staff could go on their scheduled days off, for which they were paid. These annual excursions went to a different venue every year and were most popular with the staff. Unfortunately they were once again terminated when the Transport Department was taken over by the West Midlands Passenger Transport Executive in 1969.

With the introduction of the Road Traffic Act 1930 which, amongst many other regulations, controlled and limited bus drivers' hours of work, a Schedules and Traffic Office was created under the charge of Mr R. Chaplow. The Act also stipulated the mechanical efficiency and safety of the buses and this required more garage staff as vehicles had to be inspected every twelve months by a Government Inspector and re-certified as being fit for passenger service every five years. I may add that these inspections were extremely thorough and searching and on these occasions the garage staff really did a wonderful job of work in turning out the vehicles in tip-top condition.

With the opening of the new bus garage, a regular night shift of engineers and cleaners was set up; the foreman, Sam Turton, with Bert Beckett and other fitters and cleaners servicing the buses for the following day. As not all the petrol-engined buses had electric starter motors fitted, it required sheer brawn to get them going in the mornings, especially during the winter months. Each morning a number of "spare" drivers and conductors booked on at 5 a.m. and were detailed to start all the bus engines before half past five. This was done by two men on the starting handle, one using the right hand and the other left hand (I liked the left hand) and another man on carburettor so that on first firing he kept the engine going. Woe betide him if he didn't! The man on the carburettor always carried a supply of matchsticks so that once the engine was running he could place one under the carburettor adjusting screw so that the engine would tick over rather fast. After some time the engine became very hot and then it was his job to go round the fleet and switch them all off. When the regular drivers reported for duty, they would find warm engines which could be started without difficulty and go out on service on time.

Eventually, a Whipple starting engine was acquired by the Department. This was a mobile petrol engine with a twin horizontally-opposed engine, which, operating through a clutch and cardan shaft that fitted to a special attachment on the bus starting handle, turned the bus engine. This required only two men to operate; one on the Whipple and the other on the carburettor and little or no manual effort.

Another innovation which was installed went by the name of Rad-right. This apparatus consisted of a gas-fired steam boiler from which overhead insulated pipes carried steam to flexible hoses which hung from the roof girders. These hoses could be plugged into a special fitting on the bottom tanks of the bus radiators, so supplying a small

8

quantity of steam at low pressure to the engine water which prevented freezing during the night and assured easier starting in the morning. This was before the days of anti-freeze, so from October until the end of March every year all radiators were half blanked out and the water hoses were wrapped with strips of felt to afford them some protection and avoid the problems of burst radiators and frost damage to the engines.

During the 1930s an innovation was brought in which involved considerable co-operation between the Transport Department and the General Post Office. This was the fitting of a post-box on the nearside mudwing of certain buses. The post-box was attached to the vehicle by a specially fitted stanchion. A postman met the 7.45 p.m. bus from Dartmouth Square on route 8 at the General Post Office and fitted the post-box securely into position on the stanchion by means of a self-locking device. People wishing to post letters stood at the various bus stops along the Stone Cross route and posted their letters either on the outward journey or on the 8 p.m. return run. When the bus returned to the main West Bromwich Post Office, a member of the postal staff removed the letter box. This gave the residents of at least part of the town the benefit of a later letter collection and became a most popular facility which was only discontinued in 1939 owing to the outbreak of the Second World War.

In 1937, various events in the town were arranged to mark the Coronation of King George VI and the Transport Department decided to produce an illuminated bus as its contribution. A single-deck bus was taken out of service and the coach builders provided panels all round the vehicle showing various patriotic emblems; these were painted by George Knight, one of the fitters. The bus also had a large crown on the roof also constructed by the coach builders and the whole outside of the vehicle and the crown were lit by hundreds of twelve volt lighting bulbs. In order to provide enough electricity for those many lamps, the seats were removed from the interior of the bus and a petrol engine installed which drove two shaftings which were the length of the bus. From these a number of bus dynamos were driven so providing enough power for the lamps. The bus was driven by volunteers – fitters, electricians and bus drivers – for the seven evenings of Coronation week when it toured the various suburbs of West Bromwich. It was acclaimed a huge success and, when the bus was stripped of its decorations, the crown was stored on the roof of the inspectors' office inside the main garage where it remained for many years.

It was also during this period that Ernie Crump, who wrote the article in the "Black Country Bugle" mentioned earlier, was, at his own request, transferred from his position as a bus inspector. He had been promoted to this position, together with H. Holland, in the early 1930s but became a fitter in the garage owing to health reasons.

It was in 1934/35 that I passed my P.S.V. driver's examination and was put on the drivers "spare list". This consisted of doing all sorts of duties including driving buses, Corporation cars, refuse bin wagons, electricity vans; in fact, any job which had to be covered due to sickness or holidays. Whilst on the spare list I was only guaranteed forty hours per week against the standard 48 hour week and, of course, on bottom rate drivers pay. However, the time passed quickly and eventually I was placed on the regular bus drivers' rota.

I well remember the drivers P.S.V. badges at the time; these were red, oval, metal enamelled badges with a small leather strap to button to the tunic. Mine was numbered D577, 'D' being the symbol of the West Midland Traffic Commissioners Area of the Ministry of Transport. After a short time the Ministry decided to change the design of the badge, for it had been found that when a bus driver was swinging a bus to start it, that is, using the starting handle at the front of the bus, the badge could swing round and injure the driver's face.

Throughout 1937 and 1938 there were rumours in the air that buses would replace the Birmingham Corporation tramcars which ran on the 74 and 75 routes through West Bromwich from Birmingham to Dudley and Wednesbury via Carters Green. The agreement under which Birmingham Corporation ran its trams on behalf of West Bromwich was due to expire on the 31st March 1939. The state of the tram track, which a few years earlier in the Hill Top area had been quite appalling, but had been replaced, was now in certain places again becoming in need of urgent replacement. The section from the Hawthorns through West Bromwich High Street to Carters Green required a £75,000 investment and the option to replace it with either trolleybuses, as favoured by West Bromwich, or by motor buses was becoming urgent.

By the end of 1937 it was decided that the trams would have to go and that they would be replaced by a jointly operated motor bus service of both West Bromwich and Birmingham Corporations. West Bromwich wanted to bring the closure date forward to 31st December 1938 as their agreements for operation in Wednesbury and in Dudley expired then but this decision was made too late for Birmingham to get all the replacement buses delivered in time, nor was it possible to speed up the alteration of Birmingham's Hockley depot. Tramway operation therefore had to continue until 31st March 1939.

After Christmas 1938, many new drivers and conductors were recruited and had to be trained for the new operation. Thirty-one new Daimler buses were on order so that West Bromwich could take its share of the running of the new services. In addition to the extra platform staff, more garage engineers, cleaners and clerical staff had to be employed. I suppose that, in all, about 150 new staff in all were recruited to the Transport Department at this time.

It was necessary to increase the garage capacity to cope with the enlarged fleet. This extension, when first built, had the distinction of having the largest uninterrupted roof span in the Midlands. This was particularly useful when manoeuvring buses in the garage and not having to worry about hitting roof support pillars. This building also included several more service pits linked by a sunken workshop area so that the fitters could work on the same floor level when repairing or replacing a chassis or engine component. A large canteen, sheet metal shop, a large body shop, an electricians room, a trimmers room and a large lecture room were also accommodated on the new extension.

There was a a lot of work to be undertaken before the changeover, such as new rosters for the driving and conducting staff, and the preparation and publication of timetables for the new bus services. Interestingly enough, the fares for the new bus services showed no increase over those charged on the trams which they replaced, although, as was common with tramway replacements, the number of request stops along the route was reduced quite a bit.

Added to my own job at this time was the supervision of putting up all the new bus stops along the routes, as well as queue barriers at the busier points. In connection with this, I was also responsible for the removal of all the old tramway stop signs, most of which could not be removed until the trams had actually stopped running on the final night of operation. I also was placed in charge of the production of all the new bus timetables and all the publicity. This of course had to be printed and then pasted in the windows of every bus so that the passengers would become aware of the impending changeover.

From that time onwards, my job as Traffic Inspector included the task of seeing that all bus stops were in good condition and that all the public timetables were up to date. If they were in any way wrong, I had to go out along every route either correcting or replacing them.

The final preparations for the new bus services took place in the last week prior to the abandonment. For instance, the job of erecting new bus stops was completed at 6 p.m. on Saturday 1st April 1939, when Bill Downes, myself and several others celebrated at the corner of Horseley Heath and Sheepwash Lane, Great Bridge. Not far from there was the Ryland aqueduct where a canal spanned the roadway at Dudley Port. This was a low, arched, brick-built bridge through which trams and buses could only just pass by using the middle of the road. Compulsory red bus stops were erected on both sides of the bridge so that bus drivers had to stop their vehicles before proceeding beneath and make sure that other vehicular traffic was not approaching or over-taking so that they could use the centre of the carriageway. White lines were painted on the road to help them in this matter.

In order to give the necessary ticket inspection and general supervision on these two important services, several more traffic inspectors were promoted from the driving ranks. These were C.Baggott, W. Bradley, J. Brooks, F.Horton, George R.Jones and C.Ratcliffe.

Some of the names of the traffic staff employed at this time, as far as I can remember them, were bus drivers Jack Abbotts, E.W.Barker, C.Beard, H. Birch and his brother Stan, H.Fenton, Sid Hall, H. Jones, G. Horton, C.King and his brother Harry, G.Morris, C.Mullard, George Mumford, Charlie and "Snowy" Payton, W.Stanton, George Truby and W.Richards.

WARTIME MEMORIES

Although the prospect of the outbreak of war had been looming throughout the summer, when it actually began to look inevitable, at the end of July, it did rather catch the bus operators away from the Capital a little unprepared. As soon as war was declared on Sunday 3rd September 1939, the first inconvenience was the immediate introduction of the blackout regulations. These were strictly enforced; not a glimmer of light was allowed to be shown anywhere except by moving vehicles. Even these were only allowed side lights of half an inch diameter, with the use of headlights being forbidden. Buses had their interior lights so heavily masked that it was all but impossible for the conducting staff to do their job at night. After much complaining, the conductors were issued with a battery-operated torch that was fitted with a masked hood. This deflected the light downwards and enabled the conductor to take fares and issue tickets at night without any light showing upwards.

The operation of the bus services by the crews during the hours of darkness became very onerous, particularly when the night was cloudy or if the weather had become inclement and there was no moon. It was particularly difficult driving a bus in the pouring rain with no street lights or vehicle lights to be of any assistance to the driver. As may be expected the accident rate increased enormously. Similarly, Oak Lane garage had to remain in complete darkness throughout the night hours and until the carpenters could erect a double door arrangement, in addition to the normal window blackout, all lights had to be extinguished when buses were coming in or out during the hours of darkness.

Another early effect of the war was the immediate call-up of all men on army reserve, including, for some months, the manager Mr Witcomb Smith and those on Territorial Service. This meant trying to recruit more bus drivers and conductors. As the months passed by more and more conductors were called to the colours and so began the recruitment of women for bus conductresses. I was placed in charge of the training of these women for some time and I suppose many hundreds passed through the school but the names of many of them now escape me.

P.S.V. drivers were exempt from military service, so, in order to maintain the necessary strength of staff to continue the services, men were directed by the Ministry to work as bus drivers. The town's ambulances had been stationed at Oak Lane garage for many years, and, on instruction of the Ministry, four single-deck buses were taken out of service for the duration of the war and converted by the coach builders to ambulances by removing the seats and installing stretchers and other necessary equipment. Bus drivers were instructed in First Aid and then became air raid personnel as required. The lecture room in the new section of the garage was equipped with bunk beds and so many men detailed each night to report for this type of work in case of enemy air raids. Later in the war, fire watching became compulsory because the enemy were using so many incendiary devices, men on this duty were similarly accommodated. The canteen, which was situated beneath the lecture room, became an important part of the garage, being open twenty hours of the day.

Within a few weeks of the outbreak of war, the Government introduced fuel rationing which caused the Corporation to drastically curtail bus services outside the peak services.

On Saturday 27th January, 1940, one of the worst blizzards of the century swept across the country. There was no real advanced warning as there were no up to date weather forecasts as there are today. The snowfall continued throughout Sunday and when I went out at 4 o'clock on the Monday morning, on the early duty, the snow was waist deep. The prospect of even starting a normal bus service was looking extremely remote. Amazingly, we got all the buses out onto their routes by about 7a.m. but soon the first reports of buses becoming marooned in the deep snowdrifts began to come in.

This situation was not unique to West Bromwich as the whole country had been caught out by the appalling weather. All forms of transport were paralysed for several days, which at least had the effect of taking the public's mind off the rigours of the war, although, only a few days before the big freeze, food rationing had been introduced. The transport authorities had virtually no available snowploughs or gritting lorries and to start with every local authority had to find their own answer to opening up the more vital main road links. Eventually, by a

14

lot of hard work, services returned to normal although the snow took months to disappear.

The experience of this awful weather and the problems it caused us on the operating staff led us to the conclusion that a small number of buses should be available as snowploughs in case of future bad winters. This led to five or six buses being fitted with snowplough brackets, so that the plough could be fitted in a very short time in the event of snow. The buses were then sent out on special snowplough "routes"; the specially trained drivers followed a set route which eventually resulted in all roads used by buses being cleared of deep snow.

Early in 1940 it was decided by the Transport Committee to allow the operation of a staff bus in order to take members of the Transport Department to and from work. The two new Jensen bodied single-deck Daimlers 106 and 107 were used on this duty. For many years, starting during the war, these two buses were driven by Drivers G.Horton and H.Jones who continued with this largely unsung but most important duty until they retired. They came on duty at 11 p.m each evening and were available throughout the night for this extra duty until 7 a.m. on the following morning when they became available for normal driving duties until 9 a.m. These staff buses ran on two separate routes covering the outer suburbs of the borough and observed timing points at several locations. They both left the garage at a few minutes after midnight and on their two early morning runs, they arrived at Oak Lane garage at 4.20 a.m. and at 5.30 a.m. These buses were very much appreciated by the employees particularly during inclement weather, as unlike persons with indoor jobs they were unable to change into dry clothes.

During the Spring of 1940, many hundreds of schoolchildren were evacuated from West Bromwich. The bus fleet was used to take the children from specific pick-up points to the nearest appropriate railway station, from where the children were taken to the countryside well away from the possibility of air raids. There were many tearful scenes as children had to leave their parents behind, usually for the first time. All of the children were labelled, and carried their hastily packed, heavy suitcases in one hand and rather menacing gas-mask cases around their shoulders. I was in charge of many of these convoys of Corporation buses. Some went directly by road to their destinations, often many miles into the quieter distant parts of rural Staffordshire in order to find what were considered safer quarters.

When the Local Defence Volunteers (LDV) force was formed immediately after the retreat and evacuation of our armed forces from the beaches of Dunkirk, practically the whole of the employees joined and a Company was formed at the garage. Unfortunately, it was not so surprising that after a period of time, most of the workforce had resigned due to their long normal working hours. Virtually everyone worked a seven day week, plus additional time during the week when the need arose. This meant that quite often the staff were continually working seventy hour weeks. This was not just the usual clocking on and off at regular times but involved shift work. This could mean early or late duties, split duties and even three timer duties. Even when off duty men suffered from a lack of rest when there were air raids or air raid warnings.

With the reduction of men in the LDV, which was later known as the Home Guard, those men still involved were transferred to the Drill Hall at Carters Green. I found this most useful as I lived nearby and was able to do my two compulsory drills each week, one on a Sunday morning and the other during the daytime when I acted as driver to one Captain Wright.

A trailer fire pump was purchased by the Transport Department and a reserve supply of water obtained by the construction of a large underground tank at the rear of the garage. This formed an emergency supply in case of the water mains being destroyed by enemy action. Volunteers for fire fighting at the garage were trained by the local fire brigade staff. From the volunteers, seven fire officers were appointed, one fire officer per day. They were to take charge of events in case of air raid damage until the regular fire brigade arrived. I became one of the fire officers and I had to do one turn of duty per week as one of the trained fire officers with a dozen fire watchers. I reported on duty at 7 p.m. and usually remained on duty until 4 a.m. the next morning when my normal bus duties started, subject to any enemy action.

As it happened, West Bromwich was comparatively fortunate during the war, for although some bombing did take place as the town's factories were a target, the amount of damage was fairly minor when compared to that received by Birmingham and Coventry. The transport department was virtually untouched. Oak Lane garage was only slightly damaged by a bomb blast and in one corner a piece of bomb shrapnel put a hole in the wall of the General Manager's office on the night of Tuesday 19th November 1940.

The air raids did teach us a lesson, particularly after the bad raids on nearby Birmingham, which destroyed both buses, at Hockley on the night of the 22nd November 1940 and later trams, at Miller Street on 9th April 1941. The Hockley raid affected the joint operation of the bus service between Birmingham and West Bromwich. The direct hit on the garage destroyed six virtually new buses and put another fourteen off the road for a lengthy period while their chassis were repaired and replacement bodies obtained.

As a result of this, our buses were only refuelled and serviced at Oak Lane garage. Once this was done, the vehicles were dispersed and parked in the surrounding streets during the hours of darkness. It meant that if the garage were to be hit by a bomb, there would be comparatively little disruption to the bus fleet. Dispersal did cause a lot of problems to the garage night staff. In blackout conditions, they had to park the buses in the late evening or when the services finished and then go and collect them again the following morning, again, if it was winter, during hours of darkness. I often wondered how many of the local residents ever got any sleep, what with the worry of air raid alerts and the engines of the dispersed buses being run half the night outside their houses in the winter months to prevent them from freezing up.

The war years were a particularly difficult time for the Transport Department and these early years, with the threat of bombings and invasion, were probably the worst. Gradually life settled down to a pattern of work which was always relying upon ingenuity to keep the wheels turning. Old buses were reprieved from the scrap merchant and kept running for as long as possible, which usually meant when the last of the cannibalized spares ran out. Everything was done on a "shoestring". Wartime destination blinds were of a much poorer quality but we were grateful for anything new, even if the service routes on the blind were in the incorrect order.

The bus services themselves were actually little changed by the war. Only the Kingstanding and Sutton route was abandoned. The main alterations involved curtailments of normal services, especially in the evenings.   For instance, the last 220 bus from Dartmouth Square to Bearwood left at 8.55 p.m. instead of the pre-war time which would have been over two hours later.   Unnecessary journeys for pleasure, for example, to the cinema were just not made anymore.   Extra journeys on scheduled bus services had to be concerned with the war effort and the luxury of using a bus for pleasure was regarded in a very poor light. The frequencies were altered to reflect the changing pattern of use of the buses.   Early morning workman's services started much earlier in the morning and workers journeys on Sundays were introduced.   The 74 route now started at about 5.20 a.m. on a Sunday morning which was nearly three hours before the pre-war equivalent.

Through all this fuel was being heavily rationed and supplies of petrol and diesel fuels had to be conserved, yet at the same time services had to be maintained.   The Corporation was even under threat of having to run buses on producer gas, but fortunately this never materialized.

The length of time between vehicle overhauls was at first lengthened and then virtually abandoned, as buses were placed in service provided that they were safe to drive and would not break down before the end of the shift.   It was some comfort to know that so much of our bus fleet was virtually new when war broke out, although by 1945 even the still fairly new Daimler COG6's were in dire need of major overhaul.   Any repainting was only to repair accident damage and many of the "Austerity" Daimlers which were delivered between 1943 and 1945 came painted in battleship grey.   Many of these also came with the added delights of wooden slatted seats and only one pair of opening windows in each saloon.   While the public suffered in silence, presumably only too pleased to be able to actually get on a bus at all, we were also glad of the extra buses as, by about 1943, the strain on our resources was getting to breaking point with the demands being made on delivering workers to the munitions factories scattered in and around the Borough.

About 1944 special passes were introduced for key shift workers in the local factories which were at that time working flat out on wartime munitions work.   They had to travel to or from their places of employment on the late evening buses which were much reduced during the war.   These passes ensured that they were allowed to board these buses in preference to other passengers who were out socializing.

18

This caused a few grumbles but was generally accepted without causing too much of a problem.

As the war progressed in Europe and the possibility of air-raids became less of a threat, the Government slightly relaxed the blackout regulations and allowed the front indicators of buses to be illuminated, although the effect was somewhat dim! Despite the minimal improvement, this extra destination-box lighting was a boon to passengers because they were once again able to see at night where the bus was going. This was particularly useful when a bus stop was being used by a number of different services, for example in West Bromwich High Street.

Another concession was that the interiors of buses could be illuminated, but here again the lighting was dim. The light bulbs were covered at first by a cardboard inverted cone that lit up the ceiling of the saloon and put a pinpoint of light in the vague direction of the passenger seated below. These cardboard cones were soon damaged by the crews as they attempted to get more light into the gloomy saloons and they were quickly replaced by more substantial metal ones. Yet despite their shortcomings, even this amount of lighting within the buses was a tremendous boon and morale booster to the platform staff and the passengers alike. For the first time in four years those working and travelling at night in the Corporation's buses were able to see what they were doing instead of fumbling in the dark.

Hostilities in Europe came to an end on 8th May 1945 and V.E. Day was a public holiday. On this day the bus services in West Bromwich had to be suspended as it became impossible to operate on the routes because of the celebrations going on.

The war finally ended in August 1945 and West Bromwich Corporation Transport Department had lost seven members of its staff killed on active service. The Transport Committee had a memorial tablet made which was fitted to one of the brick pillars at the entrance to Oak Lane garage. Some years later, unfortunately, the tablet was stolen, presumably for its scrap metal value. The Transport Committee replaced it and installed it in a place of honour inside the office entrance hall at Oak Lane garage. The wording of the plaque was as follows:

IN MEMORY OF EMPLOYEES OF WEST BROMWICH CORPORATION
TRANSPORT WHO GAVE THEIR LIVES IN THE WAR OF 1939-1945.
JACK CLEMENTS
ALBERT FORRESTER
ARTHUR HAYNES
JOSEPH JERRISON
ALFRED HENRY ERNEST JONES
HERBERT JAMES WHITEHOUSE
JOHN BATES WOOLDRIDGE
Unveiled by the Mayor, Alderman G.C.W. Jones J.P.
Chairman of the Transport Committee
Wednesday, February 9th, 1949.

I can remember the names and most of the faces of the stalwarts of the wartime Transport Department who maintained the services throughout the hostilities. Among the drivers were F.Adams, J. Aston, G. Atterbury, B. Barker, H. Bates, T. Beard, J. Benbon, H. Birch, T. Birkitt, B. Brewer, A. Cammies, J. Cashmore, E. Cleaton, H.G. Dicken, G. Evans, G. Fletcher, J. Gordon, S. Hall, J. Harris, D. Johnson, C. King, H. King, W. Kramer, H. Leach, W. Lewis, J. Longhurst, F. Machin, A. Martin, H. Mason, G. Mullard, C. Paynton, W. Paynton, E. Raybould, W. Richards, H. Shelley, J. Slater, W. Stanton and E. Whitehead.

The back platform staff I can remember were H. Armstrong, J. Aspbury, R. Benger, Miss Brotherton, T. Burns, Miss I. Coates, Mrs L.Hunt, J.Hamblett, Mrs O.Jesson, F.Morris, Mrs C.Morris, Mrs I. Morgan, Mrs H. Owen, Mrs O. Peters, Mrs Pratt, Mrs Reynolds, Ruby and Olive Richards, J. Taylor, S. Tongue, B. Walters, B. Woodall and Miss F. Wright.

The traffic inspectors all came under the jurisdiction of the Chief Inspector H.Holland. The other Inspectors included C. Baggot, H. Bowater, W. Bradley, J. Brookes, J.V. Cale, F.G. Green, W. Holyhead, F. Horton, S. Jones and E. Ratcliffe.

In the garage at this time were W. Ashby, J. Elcock, H. Groves, H. Hawkes who worked in the stores, G. Pester, J. Styles who was a trimmer, S. Trow, a painter, and H. Wilkes, who was also a storeman. The three ambulance drivers were T. Delamere, P. Ellis and A. Parkes.

Of course there were many more whom I cannot remember but it was a long time ago.

Not a bus and not even West Bromwich but the mainstay of the "main line" routes from 1924 to 1939, Birmingham Corporation tramcar 545 passes the junction of High Street and Paradise Street at Dartmouth Square on the last Friday of Birmingham Corporation tramcar operation on 31 March 1939. (H.B. Priestley)

This early post-war view of the High Street at Dartmouth Square shows a much more animated scene. 105, one of the 1940 Daimlers is followed by Birmingham's 281, a Leyland Titan, which is working on the 74 route from Dudley. In the distance, may be seen 63, the Weymann bodied former demonstrator of 1937, still with its non-standard destination boxes. (Commercial Postcard)

21

The original buses in the fleet were four Albion A12 chassis with 25-seat bodies built locally by W.J.Smith and painted in a two-tone grey livery. Two are seen here with the some of the staff of the Transport Department in September 1914 prior to their short-lived career until the chassis were commandeered by the War Office. The bodies were later used on Edison battery-electric and then on Tilling-Stevens TS3 chassis. (WBCT)

During the 1926 General Strike, there were neither trains nor Birmingham Corporation trams so from 5th to 11th May, West Bromwich Corporation ran an emergency service to Birmingham. Tilling-Stevens bus 3, loads outside Snow Hill Station. Just visible on the original print is the message chalked on its side-windows "TRAM FARES BIRMINGHAM – WEST BROMWICH". (WBCT, courtesy D.F. Potter)

Also at Snow Hill Station during the General Strike is Tilling-Stevens Bus 5 with its curiously curved front canopy on the locally-built Roberts body. This was the first bus to be delivered in the blue and cream livery. Behind is the 14-seat Morris-Commercial No.6. The service was run with volunteer crews and a solitary policeman appears to be supervising the situation. (WBCT, courtesy D.F. Potter)

No apology is necessary for including three General Strike scenes as views of these early buses are very scarce. Tilling-Stevens TS6 No.9, only one month old, stands fully laden outside Snow Hill Station when substituting for the Birmingham trams. This was the first full-sized bus in the West Bromwich fleet. (WBCT, courtesy D.F. Potter)

Although only having a 37 h.p. engine, this Guy BB displays an impressive frontal appearance as it stands in Barrows Street awaiting the return of its crew. Fitted with a Guy 30-seat body, bus 12 was one of three similar vehicles, numbered 11, 12 and 14. The fleet number 13 was never used! (R.T. Coxon)

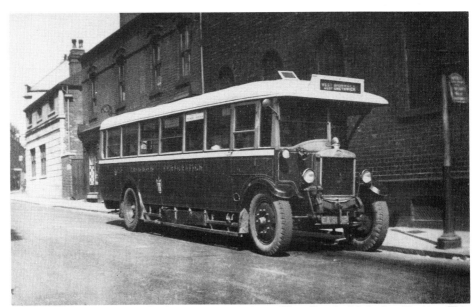

Standing in Spon Lane on the former tram service to West Smethwick is Guy No.19. This early 1930s view shows a modern-looking Guy body married to a very 1920s chassis design. Note the "Feathers In Our Cap" Red Indian radiator filler-cap mascot and the cornet shaped horn below the windscreen. (D.R. Harvey collection)

The need for small, one-man-operated single-deckers to operate over Galton Bridge at Smethwick, arose when the Carters Green to High Street Smethwick route opened on 28th July 1930. Bus 27, a rare forward-control Guy ONDF was a miniature twenty seat version of the previous five Guy FBBs, one of three purchased in November 1929, and seen here in High Street at Dartmouth Square when new. (R. Marshall collection)

In 1939, the ten year old bus 32, a Dennis E with a Dixon body stands in St.Michael's Street, West Bromwich before working on the Bromford Lane route to Oldbury. 32 led something of a charmed life surviving until 1962 when it was offered for preservation and it has been looked after ever since by Ray Coxon who, by sheer chance, took this photograph! (R.T. Coxon)

25

The only double-deck bus body to be built in West Bromwich was a speculative venture by Dixons and was fitted to Dennis Lance 42 in May 1932. The body was an excellent example of the bodybuilders' craft but unfortunately it was Dixons last body, as they closed soon afterwards. It is seen in Paradise Street about 1937. (D.R. Harvey collection)

Another local body manufacturer was W.D.Smith of High Street, West Bromwich, who finally closed down at the end of 1994. They bodied a total of six single-deckers for the Corporation. Four of them were very neatly styled Dennis Ace chassis and were given the nickname 'Flying Pigs' because of their snout-like bonnets. 46 is posed at All Saints Church prior to entering service in October 1934. (R. Marshall collection)

In 1934, W.J.Smith & Son Ltd, proprietors of Jensen Motors, bodied two Dennis Lancets with 38-seat bodywork. The second, numbered 48, is seen here outside their works carrying Trade Plates prior to delivery. The massive radiator and bonnet somewhat masked the fact that an outwardly modern bus had a chassis that was basically an upgraded model E which had been introduced some six years earlier. (WBCT, courtesy D. Phipps)

The first modern looking double-deckers were four Dennis Lances built in 1934. These had metal-framed Metropolitan-Cammell bodies with smooth sloping fronts that gave the buses their more modern appearance. Bus 52, the last of the batch, prepares to pull away from the Dartmouth Square stop in High Street in about 1948 when working the 16 route to Spon Croft. (R. Marshall)

27

Waiting at the top of Spon Lane is 1934-built Daimler 53. With a similar Metro-Cammell body to 52 (previous page), it had the advantage of being fitted with a Gardner diesel engine and was the first bus in the fleet to be so equipped. It also had a Wilson pre-selector gearbox which made the driver's duty behind the wheel far easier. (R. Marshall)

With the rain glinting on the road surface, bus 56 was photographed in Paradise Street, just off Dartmouth Square. It is another W.D.Smith bodied Dennis Ace. These little 20-seaters were used for private hires or learner duties as well as on the more lightly trafficked services. (R. Marshall)

Dennis Lancet 57, a 1936 example, arrives at Dartmouth Square on the 31 route from Wednesbury via Moorlands Estate. It was one of the two bodied by W.D.Smith and makes an interesting comparison with the earlier works view of the W.J.Smith bodied 48. This bus spent the whole of the Second World War converted to an ambulance. (A.B. Cross)

Having received its first post-war repaint, Leyland Titan 65 waits in Spon Lane while its crew sit downstairs having their break. This bus was the only one in the fleet to be fitted with a torque-converter. This gave the bus two forward gears, an indirect drive, up to about 20 m.p.h. and direct, which was the equivalent to today's overdrive. (R.A. Mills)

Standing at the All Saints Church terminus, during the First World War is the Edison battery-electric bus EA 301. It is carrying the W.J.Smith body from one of the original Albion petrol buses. The church in its rural setting, with its lychgate guarding the churchyard entrance, forms a contrast to the nearby industrial heartland of the Black Country. (Commercial Postcard)

On a snowy winter's day in 1966, two seventy-three seat Daimlers, 245 from Hamstead and 225 from Sutton load for the town centre at the concrete bus shelters outside All Saints Church. Compared to picture above, taken some fifty years before, the almost village-like look of the area has been lost but subsequent traffic management schemes have today brought many further changes to the junction. (D.R. Harvey Collection)

30

Dennis Lance 50 stands at All Saints Church terminus on 10th September 1934. It will work through the town centre and on to Lewisham Road Smethwick via Halfords Lane. This cross-town route was reduced to peak periods only the following Spring when the 220 service to Bearwood was introduced. (J.L. Brown)

Perhaps the most important pre-war bus purchased by West Bromwich was number 64. This was a Daimler COG6 with an Metro-Cammell 56-seat body of a similar style to some which had been recently purchased by Edinburgh Corporation. One of four vehicles bought for evaluation before deciding on the tram replacement order, this was the combination that won the order. It is seen in Paradise Street in this early post-war view. (R.A. Mills)

31

Unique among purchases by West Midland operators before the Second World War was this A.E.C. Regent, with a Charles Roe 56-seat composite construction body. This stylish vehicle was one of the four purchased for the evaluation mentioned above. This official bodybuilder's photograph was taken near Leeds in December 1937, the bus entering service on New Years Day 1938. (Charles H. Roe Ltd)

Standing outside the Employment Exchange in Paradise Street when working the Stone Cross via Tantany service is Daimler 74, one of the thirty that entered service in April 1939 as part of the replacement of the Birmingham tram service. Overtaking it is wartime Daimler 124 setting off for Great Bridge via Wood Lane. In this early 1950s view, both buses retain their small 'artillery-style' headlights. (A. Ingram)

32

This view dates from about 1934. Birmingham Corporation tram 614, a Brush-bodied car built in 1920, has just left the stop at the Farley Clock Tower at Carters Green on its way from Wednesbury to Birmingham on service 75. Behind the clock is the Wesleyan Chapel, built in 1876 and was distinguished by its nine tall Gothic arched windows. After being used as a warehouse for many years the chapel was finally demolished in 1970. (Commercial Postcard)

At first glance not a lot has changed in this picture of around 1950 showing 1939 Daimler number 86 about to leave Carters Green for Dudley. The excellent display of flowers has appeared and the substantial tram shelter has disappeared whilst the telephone call box has been updated and the street lighting modernized. (Commercial Postcard)

33

Bus 75 crosses the industrial railway siding when working the peak hours service to Greets Green via Albion. This 1958 view shows a changing industrial landscape with a new factory to the right mixed with Victorian houses and factories. Today the area has been completely redeveloped and there remains nothing recognisable from this picture. (R.F. Mack)

The pre-war Daimlers put in sterling service, in some cases for up to twenty-four years. 81 is seen here in a mid-1950s view, waiting in Bearwood Bus Station to return to West Bromwich via Halfords Lane. The bus is by now carrying advertisements to raise revenue for the operator. The registration plate has apparently disappeared at some stage and been replaced by a painted registration mark. The bus behind is 176 working the 221 service. (A.B. Cross)

34

The second joint route to Bearwood was the 221 and, like the 220, Midland Red and the Corporation each provided half the vehicles. The company built their own chassis and the Brush company built this body. EHA 262 (fleet number 2130) dates from 1938 and is standing at the Lower Queen Street terminus in about 1955. The Kings cinema can be seen in the background. (A.B. Cross)

On a damp day in the late 1950s, Daimler 84 climbs Soho Hill, Hockley followed by an Austin A30 car and a Bedford articulated lorry. 84 had its original body burnt out by an electrical fault at Dudley Port in April 1943. Its replacement was the first post-war body to be built by Metro-Cammell in June 1946. Route 72 was entirely within Birmingham but West Bromwich worked one or two morning peak trips to maximize vehicle use. (R.F. Mack)

35

Daimler 88 was one of four of the tramway replacements which was rebuilt by the Corporation's body repair section in the 1950s. Of these only 77, 88 and 96 received this amount of rebuilding with new body framing and radiused windows resulted in virtually a new body. It is seen towards the end of its career relegated to tuition duty near Oak Lane garage. (R.H.G. Simpson)

The last pre-war order to be delivered consisted of two Jensen bodied Daimler COG5/40 single-deckers. 106 entered service in March 1940 but because of wartime difficulties in obtaining materials sister vehicle 107 was not completed until November 1940. Bus 106 is seen here in Rydding Road, Wednesbury working service 31 route on 27th May 1960. (A.F. Porter)

THE POST-WAR YEARS

After all the celebrations marking the end of the war, the bus services settled down to a little less stressful existence as the street lighting was gradually restored.   I seem to remember that one of the first tasks done to restore the buses to their pre-war state was to remove all the interior lighting masks, the headlight masks and the white edgings to the front mud-guards and platform edges.

Although the war had been won, shortages of nearly everything continued.   The rationing of food, clothing, sweets, furniture and so on lasted for several years.   The first difficulty to hit the services was an acute shortage of staff to man the buses, as men and women who had been directed by the Ministry onto the buses and did not like their job anyway, simply stayed away and their loss was felt acutely.   Another factor was that with a slow demobilization of men from the forces, their wives, who had been conductresses, left the Corporation to be with their husbands.   This, of course, was quite understandable.   The gap between was filled with a huge effort by fitters, cleaners, inspectors and office staff;   in fact anyone who had a P.S.V. badge to act as either driver or conductor.   Fortunately, some of the staff who had been called up earlier in the war began to return to their old jobs.   Among these were Bill Downes, Ben Grice, Jo Jones, George Mumford, Bill Perkins and Bill Shuker.

In order to combat this perpetual shortage of traffic staff, Inspector Green was appointed as Training and Personnel Officer. Previously, during the war years, he had been training volunteer ambulance drivers and he had the authority to pass out bus drivers as well during this period when all regulations were suspended.   After some years Inspector Bowden was also transferred from outside duties to give initial tuition to the recruits for bus driving or conducting and to complete the necessary application forms to the Ministry of Transport and other paperwork.

The actual "on bus training" for new conductors was entrusted to the more suitable full-time conductors who had the recruits for a full week. They were then questioned on the various aspects of their new job by the chief inspector before being passed to the traffic office for regular duties. The "on road" driving instruction was given by three ex-regular bus drivers, Messrs P. Steele, T. Simcox and L. Seal, up to the stage when recruits had to pass the P.S.V. driving test by the Ministry of Transport inspector. If they were successful, and they usually were as the driving school had a good reputation for excellence, the new drivers were put on route tuition on services with other bus drivers. A great deal of effort, both in time and money, was spent in training bus drivers and conductors and it was disappointing to see staff put in their resignations, particularly in the 1950s and 1960s when there was such a large turnover of personnel.

In January 1947 there began one of the most severe periods of weather to affect the country since records began. The combination of heavy snowfalls, extremely low day and night temperatures and the fact that the cold weather went on throughout February and March changed the snow into packed potholed ice on the road surface. Buses were the only real method of transport available to the general public. During the war years, the public were severely restricted in their travel; petrol rationing was still in force and such cars as were being made nearly all went towards the export drive. The majority of people were therefore still dependent upon the local bus services and the severe weather which occurred caused real difficulties to the travelling public. There were shortages of staff because of illness and difficulties in getting to work. The vehicles suffered considerably as the thick ice partially melted during the day and then froze again at night. This caused the ice on the road to become rutted and potholed and led to an alarming rate of breakage of road springs.

My job in the late 1940s and early 1950s continued much as before; new bus services were begun and gradually new buses began to arrive with more frequency which in turn began to see off the veterans of the pre-war fleet.

During the whole of my early life, the cost of living remained fairly steady, with the basic shopping commodities rarely increasing in price. After the 1939-1945 War, consumer prices began to rise. Some of the factors which caused the price rises were the demands for higher wages, the introduction of paid holidays and the annual reduction of the working week from about 48 hours to a forty hour, five day week. In order to start making economies the management began to look for

38

savings at all levels of the operational system. To increase revenue, the first alteration in fares came in April 1951, with the withdrawal of shopping returns. These were available between 10 a.m. and 4 p.m. and had been introduced in the 1920s to encourage passengers to continue to shop in the town centre as the population became dispersed from the inner areas on to the new council house estates.

In April 1952 came the first general fare increase for at least thirty years. West Bromwich had become renowned in the bus industry for the cheapness of its bus fares. Up to that time it cost the normal passenger 1d to travel one stage while the range of fares went from 1d to 4d. The early morning workmen's returns had the same price range, but were return journeys! There was a scholars return rate which went up in price from 6d per week to 9d per week. After the 1952 fare increases many of these special rates were discontinued. Fare increases unfortunately became something that was to bedevil management and passengers alike over the next few years. Fares were increased in 1956, 1958, 1961, and 1965 but West Bromwich fares still remained distinctly lower than those of the other nearby operators.

For a long time, manufacturers had been trying to produce a satisfactory machine ticket issuing system. The idea was to replace the Bell Punch system which had virtually been universal throughout the country since the 1890s. It may be necessary to explain the method of issuing tickets to the passengers. The conductor reporting for duty was given the appropriate ticket box and sufficient tickets to complete his turn on duty. There was also a ticket summary sheet which gave the total value of the various ticket denominations. The tickets were in bundles of fifties and each bundle belonged to a unique series of ten thousand tickets. This series, in turn, had its own set of serial letters, for example AB or XY. As well as all the tickets, the conductor also had in his box a ticket rack in which he clipped the individual denominations of tickets in some monetary sequence along the rack. It was from the rack that the conductor issued the tickets to the passengers. Also in the ticket box was the waybill. At the end of every journey, the conductor had to fill in the serial number of each ticket category issued. It was this important document which was checked against the money brought in for that day's duty. Finally the ticket box contained the bus running card number and the timetable, for in those days it was the conductor who was responsible for time-keeping.

The bell punch machine was quite small and enabled the conductor to punch a hole in the ticket that was being issued. For convenience, it hung on an aluminium plate and was carried on the opposite side of the body to the conductors cash bag. Both punch and cash bag were carried on shoulder straps. The bell punch was so called as a bell sounded when it was operated. This was to prevent the conductor handing over an already issued and punched ticket. The punch could not be operated unless there was a ticket inserted.

The tickets had the inward and outward stages down either side and the conductor punched a ticket to the value of the passenger's journey, at the appropriate fare stage as marked on the ticket, on one side or the other according to which way the bus was travelling. This enabled the conductor to check on people who might be over-riding. In order to keep a check on the conductor, the punch had to be returned intact at the finish of duty. To ensure that the machine was not tampered with, a special piece of paper was inserted by the ticket office staff which would be damaged if the machine was opened. Inside the punch was a register for recording the number of tickets issued and a box for holding the clippings which could be counted in case of a suspicion of fraud. The number of tickets recorded thus tallied with the number sold, when the conductor completed his ticket summary sheet at the end of his duty and returned his ticket box to the ticket office.

In order for the system to operate smoothly, two sets of ticket boxes were required which were issued on alternate days. This enabled the ticket office staff to check the boxes, re-stock them with tickets and generally prepare them for the duty turns of the following day.

The ticket office staff were responsible for the checking of the individual Bell Punch ticket machines and their boxes. They also refilled the boxes with tickets and put in the necessary way-bill forms for the following day. This was costly in labour and there were some twelve to fifteen young ladies employed in the ticket office. I can remember some of the ticket office staff amongst whom there were Lillian Frazer, B. Fullard, Doris Gynne, Lillian Haines, Rita Hall, Pat Key, B. Poulton and Miss Timmins. The introduction of a single ticket box system, which involved each conductor being responsible for their own tickets, machines and paperwork virtually reduced the ticket office staff by half.

40

In West Bromwich, the bell punch was replaced by Ultimate ticket machines in 1952. These issued from one machine, five pre-printed denomination rolls of tickets. All the tickets were numbered in the same way as the punch tickets had been. In the Ultimate machine there was a geared rod which operated a number counter which was set to denote the fare stage number. As there were three positions of the rod, the stage number could appear in one of three boxes to denote whether it was an ordinary, child or workman's fare. After the 1965 fare increase workman's concessions were withdrawn as was the return fare facility.

The machines also contained numerators to record the total sales of each denomination, making completion of waybills and the paying in calculations somewhat simpler. Originally the five values of tickets in the machines were ½d, 1½d, 2d., 2½d, and 3d. Conductors had their own individual Ultimate ticket machines and ticket boxes and were responsible for maintaining them in good working order and ensuring that they had a good supply of spare ticket rolls, which were obtainable from the ticket office. Although the issuing of tickets from the Ultimate machines sounds very complicated, the conductors became very adept with them and many preferred them to the older punch system.

I mentioned earlier that manufacturers were trying to produce suitable ticket issuing machines and several types produced by a variety of companies were tested. The Setright machine was, I believe, the most popular one. It achieved national acceptance as it could be carried by conductors, and if fixed on to a special plate, could be used for one-man operation. It was quite a small machine, having a dial on the top which the conductor turned to the required fare. A further lever was moved to select the type of ticket required, for example, single or return. After setting all the necessary details, the conductor turned a handle at the end of the machine and out came the printed ticket with all the relevant details. There were no stocks of tickets involved; all the conductor had to do was to insert a blank paper roll and all the ticket details were printed by the machine. Both Walsall Corporation and Midland Red used the Setright system while Birmingham City Transport and Wolverhampton Corporation Transport adopted the Ultimate ticket machine, as had of course West Bromwich Corporation.

The only other type of ticket machines in use at Oak Lane were the Almex type which were tried out in 1963. This machine issued a single square ticket. It was never in regular use at Oak Lane garage and was not in favour with the conducting staff. It was mainly used for statistical recording on various routes around the system.

A major change in my career took place in 1955 when I went "off the road" to an inside job at the garage when I was appointed Chief Schedules Officer.

In 1957, the retirement of the General Manager, Mr A.Witcomb Smith, was announced. He had served the Corporation since just after the end of the Great War and was a highly respected person in the transport and bus industry. He was succeeded by Mr S. Jobling who remained in the position until the formation of the West Midlands Passenger Transport Executive when he was made Northern Area Manager. Mr Jobling who had been Deputy General Manager at the time of his promotion, had been earlier appointed to that position to replace the then Assistant General Manager, Mr W. Whitwell.

By 1962 I was again promoted. I was moved further up the management structure to become the Assistant Traffic Superintendent for West Bromwich Corporation. This was a position which I retained until the formation of West Midlands Passenger Transport Executive in 1969. I had to wait until 1972 before getting a further promotion.

The next main event in my period of time of working "On The Buses" was the Golden Jubilee of West Bromwich Transport in 1964. The Corporation had been running buses since Thursday 10th September 1914 when it placed in service three of the four two-tone grey Albions. To commemorate this, the Transport Committee decided to hold a celebration dinner at the Gala Baths on 10th September 1964. As well as the Mayor and Councillors of West Bromwich, there were many important dignitaries from the Ministry of Transport and the bus industry, including the other local general managers. Trade Union representatives and long service employees at Oak Lane garage were also invited, including me. A total of some 450 people attended this prestigious function.

When Mr Jobling was promoted, his former position of Deputy was taken by the appointment of Mr N. Kay, who was known as "Danny", a nickname only used out of his hearing, of course! Mr Kay left after a few years having obtained the position of General Manager at Bury Corporation Transport. He was replaced by Mr P. Ellis who, like his predecessor, only stayed for a few years before being promoted, in this case to the position of General Manager at Morecambe Corporation Transport. The final deputy to Mr Jobling was a graduate engineer, Mr Ken Sutton, who was well known in the Corporation as he had worked for a number of years at Oak Lane garage. He stayed at West Bromwich in this capacity until the West Midlands P.T.E. took over in 1969 when he was transferred to become Deputy General Manager of the North Division based at Walsall.

The 1960s brought an increase in the demand for school bus services as the local Education Department began building large, new comprehensive schools in the Borough. The first one was Churchfields Comprehensive, which was built near to the Parish Church at All Saints. The school's population eventually reached about 1500 and they had to be transported from such wide flung places as Hamstead, Yew Tree Estate and West Bromwich itself each school day. Further comprehensive schools were built at Dartmouth High, Manor School at Friar Park and the rebuilt Grammar School at Marsh Lane which also became a comprehensive school. In order to cater for these pupils a large number of extra school journeys became necessary involving negotiations with each school concerning their own specific opening and closing times. This meant that extra vehicles had to be "on service" around 8.30a.m. for school opening and around 3.30 p.m. to bring the pupils home. This allowed buses coming off the morning peak services to do this work, while in the early afternoon the buses leaving the garage, went out a little earlier to take the school children home again before their evening peak time duty.

In 1967 after a service reorganization, the 252 service between Portland Road, Smethwick and Carters Green was extended to Wednesbury via the 29 and 31 routes. The main problem on this route was an aqueduct which carried the Tame Valley Canal over Hydes Road near Hateley Heath. This area was originally served by a single-deck operated service, the 31 route, and despite the lowering of the road beneath the aqueduct by several inches, to allow for double-deck operation, a special type of bus was necessary. Two batches of low-height Daimler "Fleetlines" were ordered and these were numbered 101 to 121. They were given white coloured steering wheels as a reminder that only this type of double-deck vehicle was permitted on the 252 service. Although still technically a joint service with Midland Red, the 252 route was now operated entirely by West Bromwich as Midland Red did not possess any low bridge type of buses.

One older Daimler CVG6 did actually manage to get under the Aqueduct Bridge! Unfortunately this was before the road was lowered for the impending new fleet and the road was still being operated by single-deckers. The bus had been working the evening Lucas Works service from Great Hampton Street in Birmingham to Wednesbury. It was apparently returning to Oak Lane garage without passengers after finishing its duty turn, when the driver thought that he would take a short cut. In the dark he forgot about the Aqueduct and opened up the roof from end to end like a sardine can. Perhaps fortunately, I have now forgotten the name of the driver.

Other office staff employed at Oak Lane at this time were the Chief Administrator, Mr J. Foster, Mr Straughan in the wages section, and the head of the stores Mr H. Hawkes and his deputy Mr W. Brown. Other people employed in the finance offices included Miss M. Foster, Mrs Goodby, Miss N. Gotham, Miss M. Hadley, K. Hoey, B. Jordan, H. Payton, D. Ridgewood, Miss D. Shrimpton, D. Smallman and Alice Wyke.

The Corporation also employed cash clerks who took the money from the conductors. The cash office was open from 9 a.m. until midnight and also had the responsibility of banking the cash. Among these were J. Coombes, B. Grice, John O'Hagan, C. Hampton, Joe Jones and Bill Perkins. Some of the inspectors also did a late night duty in the cash office.

Although the decline in passenger numbers began in the 1950s with the increase of car ownership and the availability of television, by the early 1960s, Oak Lane usually put out about 120 buses in the peak periods. In West Bromwich this was from about 5 a.m. to 9.30 a.m. and from 3.30 p.m. until about 6.30 p.m. There was also additional work to cover such as swimming baths specials for schools, school trips, the express hires to Ingestre Hall, Stafford, and the increasing demands of private hire work. Of course the regular Saturday services to and from the Hawthorns, home of West Bromwich Albion F.C., had continued since the abandonment of the Birmingham Corporation tram service in 1939. Although not the sole preserve of the West Bromwich fleet, catering for the supporters of the "Baggies" required a fairly large proportion of the Corporation's bus fleet. In the post-war years it was

44

quite common to have twenty, thirty, forty or even fifty thousand fans at home matches. I well remember one occasion in the early 1950s when the Albion played a Russian team at the Hawthorns; there was not a single bus left in the garage.

West Bromwich Corporation's buses were always immaculately kept in the almost ornate and slightly old fashioned livery of medium and light blue, relieved by cream around the windows, and lined out in gold and black.. The smart appearance of the buses was matched by the quality of their maintenance. The buses themselves were allocated to duties according to their availability. The night foreman was responsible for allocating buses to the various duties for the following morning, but of course had to bear in mind that the engineers also had their rotas for routine and essential maintenance. There was close co-operation between traffic and engineering which often meant that there were very few buses left idle in Oak Lane during the morning and afternoon peak periods. Routine maintenance usually took place between 9.30 a.m. and 4 p.m. when the engineers and bodybuilders had to have the buses ready for return to traffic. Individual vehicle docking times had to be put on a very tight timetable and it was remarkable just how much work was performed by these "backroom boys" in the six hours that was available to them and usually the bus was returned to service on time.

In addition to these duties the engineers were also in charge of all the maintenance for the other Corporation departments. When the buses moved to Oak Lane in 1930, the repair of all the Corporation's vehicles came under one roof. All the Corporation staff cars, refuse wagons (although at that time known as dustcarts), ambulances, gas and electricity department lorries, parks vehicles including the lawn mowers, and the mayoral limousine came into the garage in the winter months for overhaul and even short term storage. Including the bus fleet, at the maximum there was a total vehicle stock of over 200.

The gas and electricity vehicles disappeared after those services were nationalized and as the various other departments grew in size each section developed its own transport repair system with their own premises away from Oak Lane. Eventually, other than the Mayor's and Deputy Mayor's cars, only the ambulance fleet remained stabled at Oak Lane. Even the latter left about 1976 when the the National Health Service funded the building of a new ambulance station. This was near to the fire station at Cronehills island, adjacent to the A41 road, known as the Expressway, and more conveniently nearer to the Sandwell District General Hospital.

Of the original drivers who came with the ambulances that moved from the original station at the Hallam Hospital, I can recall E. Delamere, E. Ellis, Arthur Flavel and Albert Parkes. When an accident or emergency occurred, the call was received at the telephone office. A hooter sounded in the garage which warned the ambulance crews that they were required urgently. This also warned everyone else in the garage that there was an emergency and to give the ambulance a clear passage. Someone would be waiting at the exit from the garage to give the ambulance crew their instructions as to the whereabouts of the incident. There were some rapid departures from the Oak Lane garage!

Under the 1968 Transport Act, Passenger Transport Executives were to be set up in the major urban areas outside London. They were enjoined to "secure or promote the provision of a properly integrated and efficient system of public passenger transport to meet the needs of that area with due regard to the town planning and traffic and parking policies of the councils of constituent areas and to the economy and safety of operation".

The West Midland Passenger Transport Executive was set up as a result of that Government directive. The staff, vehicles and assets of West Bromwich Corporation Transport Department were transferred to the P.T.E. on the 1st October 1969, along with those of Birmingham City Transport, the largest operator in the area, and the two other local municipal operators, namely Walsall and Wolverhampton Corporations. The provision of Municipal Transport in West Bromwich had come to an end after fifty-five years of operation. It is interesting that the buses of West Bromwich already operated joint services with all the other municipalities that were taken over by the P.T.E. In fact one third of West Bromwich Corporation's mileage was outside the Borough boundary and buses ran into the areas of eleven other local authorities.

The Walsall, West Bromwich and Wolverhampton services were placed under the auspices of the North Operating Division, while the former Birmingham services became the South Division. In the North Division, Walsall and West Bromwich were joined to form one operating district. The main offices for this district were at St. Paul's

Street, Walsall. Life went on as normal for a while and there were no alterations to the bus services for some time while the newly created P.T.E. formulated their plans.

Mr Ron Dickinson was appointed Traffic Superintendent of this North district, while I was promoted to become his deputy. As I was familiar with the local West Bromwich area, it was arranged that I should remain in charge of the traffic duties operated from Oak Lane. My normal week consisted of going to Oak Lane garage every morning and dealing with the correspondence and any of the normal day-to-day problems which could occur. In the afternoons I went to the Walsall offices. This kept me extremely busy and often necessitated me having to go to my Oak Lane office on Sunday mornings in order to catch up with the backlog of work which had accumulated during the week.

After the takeover by West Midlands Passenger Transport Executive, a further fare rise was sanctioned in 1970, when fares were worked out on a mileage basis with a minimum fare of 4d. Certain further increases occurred at the beginning of 1971 to bring the fares into line with the new decimal coin denominations shortly to be introduced. For example the minimum fare was increased to 6d (2½p) and then on 21st February 1971 the decimal coinage system came into force on the buses and the minimum fare again went up to 3p.

On 3rd December 1973, two new districts were added to W.M.P.T.E's operating structure. These were the Dudley District and the Sandwell District. This reorganisation was a result of the purchase of the Midland Red services within the P.T.E. area. Eight garages, including Oldbury, were involved in the transfer along with 1,396 employees and 413 buses. At first sight these vehicles were possibly to be seen as an asset, as none of them was more than 14 years old. This compared very favourably with some of the vehicles inherited from the four municipalities only four years earlier. Of these, many had been over twenty years old. Unfortunately the Midland Red vehicles taken over had led arduous working lives on the hilly Black Country routes. This, coupled with the lack of investment and maintenance, led to an immediate crisis of buses available for service.

It was into this situation that I was promoted to become the Traffic Superintendent for the Sandwell District. I was responsible for the services in the whole of West Bromwich and additionally, those in Oldbury, Blackheath, Bearwood and Warley. I was therefore in charge of two garages. At Oak Lane I was in charge of the operation of some 120 buses, while at the second garage, which was the former Midland Red garage at Oldbury, I had 70 buses. The operating district had working in it about 420 drivers, plus the associated Garage and Traffic Inspectors.

As Oak Lane Garage was considered to be the main operating centre in the Sandwell District, I continued to attend my office there each morning, while my deputy was in charge in the afternoon when I tried to visit Oldbury garage. This was subject to my other duties of course. These included traffic and operations meetings, meetings with Trade Union delegates and the regular area discussions which took place at the North Division head office at Walsall. Periodically, I had to go to meetings at the P.T.E. headquarters at Moseley. In addition there were discussions with the local authorities and also with the Police. Yet again the work load was so demanding that I frequently worked on Sunday mornings when it was all "peace and quiet".

In 1976, after forty-seven years in the bus industry, all of which was based in and around the West Bromwich operating area, I reached the retirement age of sixty-five. It was with great regret that I had to say goodbye to my many friends and colleagues I had known over the years when working "On The Buses".

THE BUS ROUTES

The original bus service which commenced in September 1914 ran between All Saints Church, Dartmouth Square and Greets Green. It was rather short lived for, after one month of operation the service was suspended owing to the Albion chassis being requisitioned by the War Department for use with lorry bodies in the First World War. This bus service was restarted in July 1915 by using Edison battery-electric vehicles. After 1919, when the more reliable petrol-electric buses became available, the number of bus services gradually began to grow to reach other outlying areas of the Borough.

In 1928, when I started working for the West Bromwich Corporation Transport Department some nine service routes were in operation. Of these, eight were wholly within the County Borough of West Bromwich and the ninth was the route to Walsall.

The original 1914 route had been extended from Greets Green to Great Bridge in April 1924 and at the other end from All Saints Church to the junction of Pennyhill Lane in April 1927.

In 1920, a service was started between West Bromwich and the "Scott Arms", Great Barr. This only operated on Bank Holidays but a shortlived regular service began in December of that year. In March 1921 this was cut back to Newton and curtailed to a couple of trips on Saturdays only. The Bank Holiday service continued but daily workings to Great Barr did not finally resume until August 1925 when one of the little fourteen seat Morris-Commercials was the usual choice of vehicle; this eventually became the 5 route.

In September 1924, a Sunday service was begun between West Bromwich and All Saints Church via Tantany Estate for the convenience of worshippers attending All Saints Church and relatives visiting the nearby West Bromwich Cemetery. This special service ran until the end of December 1930.

In October 1925, another new route was introduced between Oldbury and Great Bridge; this was extended to Hill Top in November of the same year. Just two months later, in January 1926, a joint service with Walsall Corporation began, operating between the two towns via Stone Cross and Fullbrook. This was later numbered 14. In the same year a service was started between West Bromwich and Hamstead Village via Great Barr. This was extended to Holland Road in 1930. In addition a service on visiting days only was operated between West Bromwich and Great Barr Hall, later known as St Margaret's Hospital.

There were two colliery services to carry miners from the West Bromwich area. Both started from Carters Green, the one going to Hamstead Colliery, started in 1920 and was numbered eventually as the 21 route. The other miners service went to the Jubilee Colliery and started in 1927. Numbered 22 it survived until the colliery closed in 1960.

In August 1927, what was to become a most popular service was introduced between Dartmouth Square and Stone Cross via High Street, Sandwell Road, Scott Street (the Tantany Estate), All Saints and Hollyhedge Road. This service was later numbered 8. In October 1929 most journeys were extended as a cross-town route to Lewisham Road via Birmingham Road and Halfords Lane to serve new housing off Halfords Lane as well as to cater for the workpeople in that area.

In August 1928 a works service was begun between Carters Green and Foundry Lane, Smethwick, mainly for the employees of Messrs Avery's at their Soho Foundry. The works bus service could be used by other members of the public and became route 23.

When the Friar Park Estate was developed in 1929, a new service was introduced via High Street to Carters Green and then to Black Lake, All Saints and Stone Cross to Friar Park as far as the Borough boundary with Wednesbury which was on the River Tame bridge in Crankhall Lane. In those days all local authorities were very jealous of their rights in allowing passenger carrying vehicles to operate within their territory. This meant that on the Friar Park route, after passengers had alighted, buses had to run empty to the junction of Crankhall Lane and Friar Street in order to turn around and return to their terminus on the River Tame bridge.

When the Birmingham & District Company single-deck tram routes to Smethwick and Oldbury were purchased and abandoned on the 18th November 1929, the replacement Corporation bus service, later numbered 16, was operated as one route from Spon Croft to Dartmouth Square via Spon Lane and then along High Street to St Michael's Street and so on to Oldbury Square by way of Bromford Lane.

The Carters Green to High Street, Smethwick service via Roebuck Lane and Galton Bridge was started at the end of July 1930 and this later became the 24 route.

On Boxing Day 1931 West Bromwich Albion played Birmingham City and a special service was operated to St Andrews from Carters Green for the fans to travel directly to the ground without having to go by tramcar and change, though naturally a higher fare was charged to protect the trams. On 26th March 1932 the experiment was repeated when bus services were provided to Villa Park where a crowd of 51,000 saw Aston Villa beat West Bromwich Albion 2-0.

Route numbers were first used in February 1931, when the new deliveries of Dennis buses 36-38 came equipped with route number blinds. With a few exceptions, such as the second-hand purchases and some of the "Utilities", all subsequent deliveries were equipped with route number apertures.

The foundation of a most important service began in July 1932. A route between West Bromwich and Sutton Coldfield originally ran as an express service during the Summer months on Saturdays and Sundays and on Bank Holiday Mondays and Tuesdays. The service ran in this form until the outbreak of the Second World War, when it was suspended. It became a regular service in 1946 and was numbered 25.

Further routes continued to be opened or extended and in 1932 the service 2 was lengthened at both ends. The Pennyhill Lane end now went as far as Stone Cross whilst from the Brickhouse Lane end it was extended to the Market Place at Great Bridge. The 19 was also extended in October 1932 from Hill Top to Stone Cross.

A new venture started in April 1935 was a jointly operated service with the Birmingham and Midland Motor Omnibus Company Ltd (Midland Red). It operated as service 220 between Dartmouth

51

Square and Bearwood, via Halfords Lane and High Street, Smethwick. As far as Lewisham Road this followed the same route as the 7 and the latter was consequently reduced to peak hours only.

Exactly one year later, on 6th April 1936, the Circular service was introduced, using small, driver-only buses. This ran from Great Bridge through Hill Top, Hateley Heath, All Saints and Dartmouth Square before returning to Great Bridge and numbered 28 or 29 dependant upon which way round the circle it went. On the first day of March 1937, the 31 service was begun; this ran between Dartmouth Square and Wednesbury via Stone Cross and the newly developed Moorlands Estate. The No. 2 route was further extended from Stone Cross to the "Navigation Inn" on the Walsall Road in December 1937.

On 2nd April 1939, the "main line" tram services were replaced by services jointly operated by West Bromwich and Birmingham Corporations between Snow Hill Station, Birmingham, and Dudley Station (74) or the White Horse, Wednesbury (75). The tramway service numbers were retained, as they were for the short-workings between Birmingham and Dartmouth Square (77), Carters Green (73) or Great Bridge (76). Two additional numbers were invented for short journeys to Hill Top (79) and to Dudley Port (78) though it is thought that there were never any regular journeys scheduled to turn at Dudley Port.

It appears that at one time there may have been an intention to operate a regular through service between Birmingham and Friar Park since appropriate wording appeared on the 1939 destination blinds (and is being displayed by bus 60 in the back cover photograph). Except for one or two morning peak journeys which ran through from Friar Park to Birmingham and for the works journeys to and from the Lucas works at Hockley this never happened.

Under the pressures of the war, the route network remained very stable and it was not until October 1945 that expansion resumed when the Sutton Coldfield route was re-introduced as a Saturdays and Sundays only service. It was not until June 1946 that a regular daily service was instituted. Minimum fare protection was given to the Midland Red on this route between New Oscott and Sutton.

A further joint service with Midland Red began in March 1947. This was the 221 route which also ran between West Bromwich and

Bearwood but via Spon Lane and Warley, incorporating the existing Midland Red service 204 between Bearwood and Spon Croft. Yet another joint service, this time with Walsall Corporation was the 54 which started on 6th October 1947. This was formed by the diversion of alternate 14 service buses to run via Yew Tree Estate instead of Fullbrook.

The following year two further joint services were introduced; the 53 route between West Bromwich and Streetly via Great Barr, Barr Beacon and Aldridge began on 4th October 1948, jointly with Walsall Corporation and using single-deck buses. The second route ran to Wolverhampton and was operated jointly with that Corporation. Numbered 90, it began on 17th October 1948 and ran via Hill Top, Wednesbury, Moxley and Bilston. At first the 90 carried minimum fares outwards from Wolverhampton and from West Bromwich in order to discourage short distance riders.

In April 1950, the original 24 route, between Carters Green and High Street, Smethwick, became a joint service with Midland Red, was extended to Claremont Road and renumbered 252. This route was further extended to the Birmingham boundary at Portland Road in November 1952.

In November 1951 the 6 route was extended at Hamstead from Holland Road to Green Lane to cater for the new housing being built in the area. It was for the same reason that in July 1952 a new route was opened. This was the 29 service which went from Dartmouth Square to the Gough Arms, Hateley Heath.

A small, but significant route extension occurred on 27th September 1952, when the Dudley 74 route was extended from Dudley Station to a new bus station much nearer the town centre in Fisher Street. Expansion of bus services continued when in November 1953 route 2 was extended onto the Yew Tree Estate.

In 1956 the Oldbury routes were taken from the Market Place into a new bus station, but the impetus for new services was now beginning to subside. An exception to this occurred in 1960, when the 10 service was diverted away from Crankhall Road to run via Coronation Road and Park Hill to cater for residents on the newly built Woods Estate. Strangely enough, in 1970 the 11 route to Wednesbury was similarly diverted away from Crankhall Lane to Woods Estate which resulted in part of Crankhall Lane no longer being served by any sort of bus service.

In June 1963, as a result of further council house construction on Charlemont Farm, a new bus route was introduced from Dartmouth Square. In order to serve that estate, the half hourly frequency on the No. 8 route to Stone Cross via Tantany was withdrawn and replaced by a new Charlemont Farm service. Gradually as the estate was opened up with new housing construction, so the bus terminus gradually moved into the estate from the original terminus at Beacon View Road to the later terminus at Windmill Crescent and the frequency of the service was increased. This new terminus also served the new, private housing development at Bustleholme Mill Estate, which lay on the far side of the Birmingham-Walsall railway line.

The 31 route between West Bromwich and Wednesbury by way of Moorlands Estate had always been a poor route in terms of its revenue and so in 1967 the area's bus services were completely re-routed. The 29 route to Hateley Heath and the 31 service to Wednesbury were both withdrawn and replaced by an extension of the 252 service from Carters Green to Wednesbury by way of the former 29 route to Hateley Heath and then along Wyntor Lane and Ryddings Lane picking up the old 31 service along its former route via Aqueduct Lane into Wednesbury.

Another joint service was initiated in May 1967. This time it was with Midland Red and was an extension of certain journeys on the No. 2 route from Great Bridge via St Marks Road, Princes End, Coseley and then into Wolverhampton. This route was numbered 268. Short workings went as far as Princes End and became the 2T, while the number 2 was retained for journeys between Yew Tree Estate and Great Bridge only.

The final significant change before the change to P.T.E. control was also the first introduction of one-man operation. Service 28 (Circular) was discontinued and 19 (Stone Cross-Great Bridge-Oldbury) was reduced to peak hours only. In their place were new services 20, 40 and 41. 20 ran roughly in the form of a figure six, from Stone Cross via Hateley Heath, Hill Top, Great Bridge, Albion, Dartmouth Square back to Heath Lane terminating at the Gough Arms. Routes 40 and 41 both ran from Dartmouth Square to Great Bridge via Hateley Heath and Hill Top. 40 ran out via Heath Lane but back via Whisty Estate and then out via Golds Hill but back via Dial Lane whilst 41 did the opposite. In order to minimize boarding times, fares were simplified at the same time to 3d and 6d only with self-service ticket machines available for 6d passengers with the correct money.

ROUTE NUMBERS.

No.   *Route.*

1. DARTMOUTH SQUARE—ALL SAINTS CHURCH.
2. PENNYHILL LANE—GREAT BRIDGE (Through Service).
3. ALL SAINTS CHURCH—GREAT BRIDGE.
4. DARTMOUTH SQUARE—GREAT BRIDGE.
5. GREAT BARR (Scott Arms).
5A. NEWTON.
6. HAMSTEAD.
6A. GREAT BARR HALL.
7. STONE CROSS—DARTMOUTH SQUARE—LEWISHAM ROAD.
8. DARTMOUTH SQUARE—STONE CROSS.
9. DARTMOUTH SQUARE—FRIAR PARK via TANTANY.
10. DARTMOUTH SQUARE—WEDNESBURY via TANTANY.
11. DARTMOUTH SQUARE—WEDNESBURY via BLACK LAKE.
12. DARTMOUTH SQUARE—FRIAR PARK via BLACK LAKE.
14. WALSALL.
15. BROMFORD LANE.
16. SPON LANE and BROMFORD LANE (Through Service).
17. SPON LANE.
18. OLDBURY—GREAT BRIDGE.
19. OLDBURY—GREAT BRIDGE—HILL TOP.
20. GREAT BRIDGE—HILL TOP.
21. HAMSTEAD COLLIERY.
22. JUBILEE COLLIERY.
23. FOUNDRY LANE.
24. CARTERS GREEN—HIGH STREET, SMETHWICK.

Route numbers were allocated in 1931 and first appeared in the timetable for February that year, from which the above list is reproduced.

All communications to be addressed Regional Transport Commissioner. No individual should be addressed by name.

Telegraphic Address:
"TRANSCOMD, BIRMINGHAM."
Telephone No.: BIRMINGHAM
CENTRAL 7442

MINISTRY OF TRANSPORT,
REGIONAL TRANSPORT
COMMISSIONER
YORK HOUSE,
GREAT CHARLES STREET,
BIRMINGHAM, 3.

ase quote in any reply:
D.988.

Your reference is:
AWS/JMS+

31st July, 1941.

Dear Sir,

<u>Stage: Market Place, Great Bridge - Stone
Cross Inn, Stone Cross.</u>

I am directed by the Regional Transport Commissioner to refer to your letter of the 26th July, 1941, and to inform you that my Commissioner has given careful consideration to your request, and In view of all the circumstances he is prepared to grant a dispensation from compliance with the conditions attached to road service permit No.01115 to enable you to extend certain journeys from the Navigation Inn to the factory site near the Bull's Head.

My Commissioner notes that this extension will only be necessary on certain trips, and in view of this he does not think it necessary to amend your road service permit at the present time, but should you find that the extended journeys become a regular feature I am to ask that you will return your permit for the necessary amendment to be made.

Yours faithfully,

for Chief Assistant to the
Regional Transport Commissioner,
Midland Region.

The Manager,
County Borough of West Bromwich,
Transport Department,
Oak Lane,
WEST BROMWICH.

KJH.

RECEIVED
-1 AUG 1941

This booklet cannot attempt to record all the minor route changes and special workings which took place. During the war, some such journeys were authorized simply by an exchange of correspondence, such as the extension of some service 2 journeys to the ordnance factory near the Bull's Head referred to in the above letter.

After some years service, the chassis side-members of the single-deck Daimlers cracked and required replacement. In this scene in the works, 106 is being repaired. The new side-members are prominent and an overhauled engine hangs above, waiting to be installed before the chassis is re-united with its body, visible in the background. The cracks are clearly visible in the upper of the two old side members lying in the foreground. (WBCT, courtesy D. Phipps)

With the driver in shirt sleeves and the bonnet side open, it can be assumed that the weather was warm when this view of 105 was taken at the Bundy clock at Great Bridge. The bus is one of four extra Metro-Cammell bodied Daimlers ordered in 1939 to the same specification as the AEA-registered batch and which entered service at the end of March 1940. (R.F. Mack)

Wartime Daimler 109 waits in the High Street before continuing to Spon Croft on the 16 route.   This bus was one of the first three vehicles allocated to the Corporation by the Ministry of Supply.   The body was built by Duple of Hendon; it was delivered in April 1943 without a glazed rear emergency window.   (R. Marshall)

In order to conserve materials in wartime, only one roller blind per vehicle was permitted so that passengers are given no route number information by wartime Daimler 113 working on service 9 to Friar Park via Tantany.   Both 113 and slightly newer Daimler 126 behind, both with Duple bodies, are travelling along High Street towards Dartmouth Square and have just passed the National Provincial Bank. (A. Ingram)

At one time the Corporation had hoped to replace the trams by trolleybuses and the garage extension completed in 1939 was designed with sufficient height to permit the inclusion of overhead wiring. Buses were usually parked outside along the garage wall and here 115, another Duple bodied wartime Daimler awaits its next tour of duty. (D.F. Potter collection)

Wartime shortages of buses meant that many operators were on the lookout for extra vehicles. In 1944, West Bromwich was fortunate to find three Wolverhampton Corporation Daimlers surplus to requirements. 131 is seen here in the forecourt of Oak Lane garage soon after its 1951 rebuilding which included an Edinburgh style cut-away rear platform. (R. Marshall)

121 has just overtaken an Austin K2 van in Moor Street on its way to Oldbury via Bromford Lane. A route number box has now been added to this wartime Daimler but its offset position shows that it was not original equipment. The bridge is over the former Great Western main line, now long abandoned, but if the Midland Metro between Birmingham and Wolverhampton is ever built it will pass beneath this bridge. (R.F. Mack)

The bodies on the wartime buses were frequently made from unseasoned timber and unlike the chassis were not very durable. In 1953, the chassis of seven wartime Daimlers, including this one, were driven to the Stirling works of Walter Alexander where they were rebodied with pleasantly proportioned five-bay bodies. 122 is seen here in High Street, on the 16 route to Oldbury, with the Dartmouth Square cast-iron clock visible in the background. (R.F. Mack)

The dignified West Bromwich livery of two shades of blue, lined out, and with cream window surrounds and roof is well displayed in this view of Brush bodied wartime Daimler 120. The fleet name was later carried down to the waist rail. The bus is parked in Barrows Street in the town centre, where the department had a house utilized as a canteen. (S.N.J. White)

The first joint service with Midland Red was the 220 route. Here, the first post-war bus arrives in Paradise Street from Bearwood. 132 originally ran with the unique 1932 Dixon body but later received a new Alexander body as seen here. This bus was the first in the fleet to have the recently developed Daimler 8.6 litre engine. (R. Marshall)

61

In December 1951, the Corporation installed an Essex bus washing machine and the official photographs of the time provide excellent shots of the interior of the airy garage. This view of the washing machine in the lowered position gives the best view of the garage. The scene is dominated by pre-war Daimlers; the nearer vehicles are, from right to left, 105, 80 and 92. The chain in the right foreground is to control the water supply. (WBCT)

In this view, the washing machine has just passed the upper deck windows of bus 113, in process of being lowered and the operator has his right hand on the control buttons. Pre-war Daimler 105 stands in the queue and ex-Southdown Leyland Tiger 111 is just visible between the two double-deckers. (WBCT)

1939 Daimler number 74 awaits its turn as newer 142 receives attention from the cleaners to finish off the windows and remove any streaks after using the washing machine. The front of the bus was not cleaned by machine and had to be done with a water brush. (WBCT)

134, a 1948 Daimler, stands in High Street, with its trafficator out, about to depart for Sutton via Great Barr and Kingstanding. Very few of this style of body were built; basically a pre-war design the only other examples went to Chester and Salford Corporations. The bus behind is Daimler 151 bound for Bearwood on the 221 service. (A. Ingram)

West Bromwich's longest route was the 74 between Birmingham and Dudley. 149 looks to have a good load waiting to board at Fisher Street Bus Station, Dudley, before the bus departs on its nine mile journey back to Colmore Row, Birmingham. The conductor, with his Ultimate ticket machine, takes a breather and gazes across at the photographer as the Bundy Clock shows 4 p.m. (C.W. Routh)

Of the seven single-deck Daimler chassis ordered in 1948, five had to be kept in store as Metro-Cammell could not immediately body them. When they were eventually dealt with the chassis were lengthened to accommodate a 30-feet long body of the cut away rear entrance style that had been developed on ex-Wolverhampton 131. 153 is seen on the 252 route near Carters Green when fairly new. (Vectis Transport Publications)

Climbing up Livery Street alongside Snow Hill Station, Birmingham is Metro-Cammell bodied Daimler 139 arriving from Dudley. Behind the van is a line of Austin FX3 taxis waiting for custom from the trains whilst the car in the foreground is a 1938 Austin 'Ruby' Seven. Snow Hill Station is now completely replaced but a small piece of the original wall remains opposite Edmund Street and still proudly displays the G.W.R. motif. (Ribble Enthusiasts Club)

Early in 1952, the Corporation put into service twenty Weymann bodied Daimlers. They were the last exposed radiator buses to be built for West Bromwich. 159 turns out of Livery Street to load at the Colmore Row shelters in front of Snow Hill Station before returning to Wednesbury on joint service 75. Unloading passengers by the station entrance in Livery Street is later Daimler 184, but this time with Metro-Cammell body. (R.H.G. Simpson)

65

A representative selection of the fleet was drawn-up in the garage forecourt on the occasion of an Omnibus Society visit in 1953. Nearest to the camera is Weymann bodied Daimler 161 with, next to it, 143, a 1948 vintage Metro-Cammell bodied Daimler. Also visible are the first wartime Daimler, 113, with its utility body recently rebuilt, Leyland 65, A.E.C. 70 and a variety of single-deckers. (R. Marshall)

Not the usual environment for a West Bromwich bus and no doubt a welcome change for bus and crew, Daimler 166, rests in a rural setting. The occasion was a children's private hire, the location Romsley and the date 16th July 1955. (J.L. Brown)

West Bromwich only purchased from the Loughborough based body builders Willowbrook on one occasion. A batch of twelve vehicles, as usual by this time mounted on Daimler CVG6 chassis, were the first 60 seaters in the fleet and all entered service on New Years Day 1957. 194 turns out of Paradise Street bound for Wednesbury when still quite new. (B.A. Jenkins)

Waiting for departure time in Aldridge, in company with one of Harper Brothers ex-St.Helens Corporation A.E.C. Regents, is 199. Buses ran out via Barr Beacon on service 53, then performed a trip on local circular service 57 before returning to West Bromwich on the 53. Both routes were jointly operated with Walsall Corporation in whose "territory" Aldridge fell. (A.D. Broughall)

Passing the rows of Victorian terraces, which so typified much of the Oak Road area is Daimler 206. This 63-seater is fitted with one of Metro-Cammell's "Orion" style bodies, which, when introduced, were much criticized for their spartan appearance. These buses were the last in the fleet to be given the "Birmingham front" style of concealed radiator which incorporating the headlights within a bulbous front panel. (R. Marshall)

The first batch of 30-feet long double-deckers was introduced in November 1958. They had Metro-Cammell 73 seat bodies on the now usual Daimler chassis. With the castle as a backdrop, 215 has unloaded in Birmingham Street, Dudley. This bus was one of the first to have the later "Manchester style" concealed radiator which has the headlights mounted in the front wings. (A.D. Broughall)

68

The condition of the West Bromwich bus fleet remained very high right up to the end of "independence", even the gold lining-out being retained as part of the livery. 222, one of the 1959 batch of 30 feet long Daimlers leaves for Hamstead on Saturday 14 June 1969 . The conductor nonchalantly standing on the rear platform and looking back up Paradise Street is carrying his Ultimate ticket machine almost at knee height. (R. Marshall)

225, numerically the last of the YEA registered CVG6/30s splashes its way along Hamstead Road on service 6. Despite its destination blind, the bus is actually returning to West Bromwich via Great Barr. The buildings in the background form part of Hamstead Colliery, one of the last pits in the West Midlands to be developed and one which did not close until March 1965. (A.B. Cross)

In April 1961 the Corporation acquired from London Transport, two Guy Specials based on the Vixen chassis, with E.C.W. 26-seat bodies. They were unusual in being normal-control, bonneted vehicles. This one became number 233 in the bus fleet but the second vehicle was used by the Health Department for two years before being taken into the bus fleet as 252. 233 is seen on a Special duty in deepest suburban West Bromwich. (D. Williams)

Seen in the High Street on 22nd July 1968 is 250, one of two Leyland Tiger Cub buses with Roe bodies that were repainted in a simplified cream and light blue livery in 1967. It is working on the famous Circular route though the destination display is of no help at all to the uninitiated. It is overtaking Weymann bodied Daimler 158 which is working the "Lanes" route from Oldbury to Spon Croft. (R.F. Mack)

70

Thirty-feet long Daimler 258 turns from High Street into Paradise Street at Dartmouth Square after returning from Aldridge on the 53 route. Considering that this is a weekday picture, to judge from the shops having their blinds out, there is peculiarly little other traffic around in this late 1960s view. (R.F. Mack)

Pulling away from a stop on the Yew Tree Estate is Daimler 260. This type of Metro-Cammell bodied 74 seater had become standard in the Corporation fleet. One-Man-Operation however was becoming an economic necessity, not possible of course with this type of vehicle, so the seven members of this class, numbered 259 to 265 were the last of a long generation of front-engined, rear-entrance buses. (D. Withers)

71

Fourteen Daimler Fleetlines with Metro-Cammell 73-seat bodies were bought as low-height vehicles in order to pass beneath the 13' 9" Hydes Road bridge in Wednesbury on the extended 252 service. They were distinguished by being painted in an all-over cream livery with light blue bands and their very shallow lower saloon windows. 107 is seen at the terminus of the joint routes to Walsall in Paradise Street. (M. Fenton)

The last buses to be purchased by West Bromwich Corporation was a batch of six Daimler Fleetlines with bodies by Eastern Coachworks. 116, delivered only six months before the take-over by the P.T.E., is seen crossing Moor Street on 14 June 1969 en route for Great Bridge on service 2. (R. Marshall)

72

THE VEHICLES

When I started working for the Transport Department in 1928, they only had eleven single-deck buses. The earliest of these were the Tilling-Stevens TS3's of 1919, which had third-hand W.J.Smith bodies that had previously been on the short-lived Albion chassis of 1914 and later on the wartime Edison battery electrics. The chassis of the original Albion buses had been requisitioned by the War Department and the replacement Edisons arrived in July 1915.

These battery-electrics recharged their batteries from the mains electrical supply. This was done from street-side boxes at Greets Green Road and at Bull Street, near to the first shop on the left, which I recollect being a newsagent and stationers. As to the battery recharging facility at the All Saints Church end of the route, I have no recollection, but there must have been something there as the batteries would not have been capable of powering the bus on a return journey without a recharge. As a schoolboy I well remember these electric buses slowly crawling up Wood Lane. We had two distinct pranks; either we ran behind hanging on to the stanchions, much to the annoyance of the conductor, or we pushed the failing bus up the hill.

The Edisons were not much loved and throughout their period of operation they were dogged by battery failure, to the extent that rarely were all four in service at any one time. Despite hiring in replacements from the Midland Red, on 1st March 1918 the Transport Department was forced to state publicly that "the local bus service has suspended itself this week, by a breakdown". In April 1919, the Department was forced to state that "electric buses continue to be very unreliable and unsatisfactory. Every effort is being made to run the service, but the only course is to place petrol buses on the road."

The Tilling-Stevens were numbered 1-3, while No.4, of 1921, was a slightly modified design from the same manufacturer, being designated TS3A. The first blue and cream liveried bus in the fleet was No.5. This bus was registered EA 999, which was the first new mark to be allotted to a Corporation bus since 1914, there having been

73

no less than eleven vehicles carrying just four different registrations. No 5 was a Tilling-Stevens TS3 of 1920, which was bodied by Roberts, who was a local bodybuilder. All these Tilling-Stevens buses had petrol-electric transmission; the 40 h.p. petrol engine, mounted at the front of the chassis, drove an electric generator which supplied a series wound motor which in turn drove the worm-geared rear axle via a propellor shaft.

Buses 6, 7 and 8, were fourteen-seater one-man-operated buses mounted on Morris Commercial chassis. 6 and 8 had bodies by Dixon, the local West Bromwich bodybuilder while 7 had a Morris Commercial body. No.9 was another Tilling-Stevens petrol-electric chassis; this particular vehicle was the first forward control bus in the fleet. This meant that the driver sat alongside the engine on the off-side instead of behind it and this allowed the Dixon body to have the comparatively high seating capacity of thirty-two. This vehicle also had the distinction of having alkaline steel plated batteries charged from the main dynamo to provide electric lighting.

The next vehicle in the fleet, No.10, was a departure for the Department; it was again a Tilling-Stevens, but this time the chassis was of the low-loading type and was fitted with an orthodox clutch and gearbox. This drove the cardan or propellor shaft to the rear wheels. The dynamo was driven off the propellor shaft which of course only generated electric power when the bus was in motion. This resulted in a gradual failure of the batteries and a consequential loss of lighting, something which never occurred with No.9.

The next bus was the newest in the fleet when I arrived. It was No.11 and it was the first time that a full size bus had been purchased that was not a Tilling-Stevens. 11 was a Guy BB and was a super up-to-date bus. Like No. 10 it had forward control but the chassis was swept up over the front and rear axles, which allowed for a low floor height. This meant that there was only one step into the saloon instead of the three which were the norm for the earlier straight chassised vehicles.

No. 11 was built locally at the Guy Motors factory at Fallings Park, Wolverhampton. It was fitted with a Guy 38 bhp 4-cylinder petrol engine, cone clutch and Dewandre brakes working only on the rear wheels. The brakes were servo-assisted which did make life a little easier for the drivers. Four-wheel brakes did not become an

74

option on this particular Guy model until the following year. The bus had a Guy body that seated 32 passengers in the comparative luxury of bucket seats; it also had a driver-operated door. The next buses to arrive were virtually identical to No.11, being again Guy-bodied Guy BBs. The only oddity was that they were numbered 12 and 14, there being no No.13 on account of its unlucky connotations!

Over the next two years ten more forward control Guys were purchased, all with coachwork built in Wolverhampton by the chassis builder. They were numbered 15 to 24 and had either FBB type, or the later FC type chassis. Their seating capacity varied from thirty-four to thirty-six but periodically the seating layout and consequently their capacity was altered. In 1929 three smaller Guy ONDFs arrived, numbered 25 to 27. These were twenty seaters but surprisingly were of a forward control layout. They had Meadows petrol engines, which like their bodies and their chassis were built in Wolverhampton. These buses which were built between 1927 and 1929 were a great advance on the earlier vehicles in the fleet and were welcomed with great enthusiasm by the staff at this time.

Primarily to cater for the ex-tramway "Lanes" routes, five Dennis E type 32-seater single-deck buses were bought and given fleet numbers 28 to 32. I remember the chassis being stored in the Highway Department's yard prior to being sent locally for bodying by Dixon. One of these buses, No.32, led something of a charmed life from its first withdrawal in 1939 and has been preserved.

Three Dennis EV single-deckers numbered 33 to 35 followed. These 32-seaters were similar to the previous ones but had a much more modern look about them, having chromium-plated radiators and a less vintage appearance. Despite their looks, they still had lurch inducing cone clutches and mechanically operated four-wheel rod brakes.

The network of services to the surrounding areas was beginning to become a more complex operation. Due to the increase in traffic requirements and because of the number of passengers being carried, the department had changed its policy towards the type of vehicle which was required to fulfil all its commitments. Gone was the need for small single-deckers and even to a lesser extent full sized single-deck buses were not now needed so much as double-deckers. From about 1934 onwards, firstly Dennis Lances and then a succession of

75

Daimlers were bought which enlarged the fleet and its carrying capacity at the same time.

Buses 36 to 38 really were a breakthrough for the undertaking, as they were the first double-deck vehicles to enter service. They were Dennis HS chassis and had Massey lowbridge bodies. In this type of bus, the seating arrangements on the top-deck were back-to-back along the centre of the saloon with a walkway all the way around the perimeter. These buses were not very popular with either the crews or the passengers. The passengers disliked them because they were always hitting their heads on the lowered parts of the lower saloon ceiling and in the upper saloon shoes and toes were trodden on by other passengers passing along the gangway to gain their seats. The drivers disliked them because they were slow and underpowered; the Dennis side valve four cylinder 5.7 litre petrol engines were the same type as those found in the earlier Dennis single-deckers. They also had very heavy steering. The conductors had a difficult job collecting the fares particularly in the upper saloon.

The next two buses, 39 and 40, were identical to the earlier Dennis EV's. They were delivered in November 1930, some seven months after the previous batch. They had bodies by the same body-builder as the aforementioned 33 to 35. This body manufacturer was W.J.Smith, who were the forerunners of Jensen Motors, makers for many years of a series of luxury, high performance motor cars.

The original No. 6 was badly damaged about this time and another Morris-Commercial chassis was ordered in December 1929 to replace it. Its new body was constructed by the Transport Department which was quite conversant with the problems involved. It seems to have been rather a one-man job as it did not enter service until September 1931 and the official rolling stock register records the body make as "built by Trevor at the Garage".

Bus No. 41 was a six cylinder Dennis Lance with lowbridge double-deck bodywork by Park Royal. In this case the upper saloon had the seating facing forward, with space for four passengers on each seat and with the gangway along the offside of the bus. 41 had been demonstrated for two months from Dennis Brothers of Guildford and was mechanically a super bus. Unfortunately, the passengers still disliked the upper saloon layout which still proved to cause difficulties regarding access.

The next bus was for many years the Transport Department's most well-known vehicle. No. 42 was another Dennis Lance, but this time it was a Mark II. However its claim to fame was that it had the only double-deck body ever produced by a West Bromwich coachbuilder. It was built by Messrs. Dixons of Trinity Road, West Bromwich and had the more usual highbridge style of body seating 48 passengers. It had five large side windows and pronounced 'V' shaped upper-saloon front windows. This body was built to a very high standard, but although built as a speculative venture in the Depression years of the 1930s, its construction must have been most unprofitable. It was delivered in May 1932 and within a few months Dixons had ceased trading! The body, however, must have been quite good as after the withdrawal of 42 in 1942, it was eventually transferred to a new Daimler chassis and the ensuing combination survived until 1953, when this time the body was scrapped and the chassis was rebodied.

In February 1933 the last of the "little" buses arrived. This was 43, a Morris-Commercial RP, with another W.J.Smith body.

About this time, a company called P.E.L., which was an off-shoot of Accles and Pollock who were based in nearby Oldbury, brought out a new design of tubular-framed seating, which was the forerunner to the seats found today on modern buses. This type of seating was very strong and light, while having the added advantages of being easy to fit and more comfortable for the passengers. From the mid 1930s, I seem to remember, the bus fleet was fitted with these modern and more practical seats.

There followed on from the little Morris Commercial another double-decker. This was numbered 44 and was another Park Royal bodied Dennis Lance. Like 42 it was also an ex-demonstrator and had the London coachbuilder's standard body design. This was a six-bay construction job which seemed to fit rather uncomfortably on the Dennis chassis.

The next eight vehicles to be bought were a mixed bag from Dennis Brothers. The first two were 20-seater single-deckers numbered 45 and 46; the bodywork was by another local coachbuilder who was rather confusingly also called Smith, but this time W.D. and not W.J.! They were not forward control, but the bodywork was built very far forward so that it gave the bus a short looking bonnet. This snub-nosed appearance resulted in the buses being nicknamed "Pigs" by the drivers and the engineering staff.

Buses 47 and 48 were four-cylinder, petrol engined Dennis Lancets. They were the first of a whole series of small batches of Lancets. These had a far more modern style of W.J.Smith body than the Dennis EV's of just four years earlier. This modern body style was to be repeated with only minor modifications up to the delivery of the last two pre-war single-deckers of 1940.

I seem to remember that it was as a result of the two successful Dennis Lance demonstrators of 1931 and 1933, plus the Dixon bodied example, that the Transport Department, in the interests of standardization, purchased four more Dennis Lances. This time, though, they went to Metropolitan-Cammell, (M.C.C.W.), for the double-deck bodies, which were the first metal-framed bodies in the fleet. Numbered 49 to 52 they entered service in the late summer of 1934.

The next bus to be acquired was bus No. 53. This was the first diesel-engined bus in the fleet. It had a Daimler chassis, with an M.C.C.W. metal-framed body, but unlike the Dennis's, which were 54-seaters, the Daimler had only 48. I recollect that the upstairs seating capacity was only 22 and this reduction in capacity was to keep within the legal maximum weight after taking account of the heavier weight of the early oil engine. The engine was a seven litre, five-cylinder Gardner and a Wilson pre-selector "self-changing" gearbox was fitted with a fluid flywheel. This meant that the driver pre-selected the appropriate gear by moving a hand lever. The vehicle did not change gear until he depressed the gearchange pedal which was a floor mounted pedal where the clutch pedal would normally have been. This arrangement replaced the hard work of double-declutching whilst the pre-selection was very useful at times when both hands were desirable on the steering wheel!

The pre-selector type of gearboxes and the Gardner diesel-engined Daimler buses with which they were associated, became very popular with the Department's management as well as the staff because there was a great saving in fuel costs compared with a correspondingly sized petrol engine. The drivers liked the pre-selector boxes which made driving in traffic much easier and, by the same token, the travelling public appreciated the generally smoother ride.

The next vehicle to be delivered, No. 54 was virtually the same as 53 but the Gardner diesel engine was flexibly mounted, which resulted in a smoother and quieter ride. The main external difference was that the design around the cab, looked far more like one of the standard Birmingham City Transport M.C.C.W. bodies.

More new buses came along in 1936. Early in the year came 55 and 56, two more Dennis Aces, with petrol engines and W.D.Smith 20-seat bodies. These were virtually identical to the two delivered in 1934. In August and September we had a quite large number of buses come into the fleet. 57 and 58 were two more Dennis Lancet single-deckers, this time with 37-seat W.D.Smith bodies of quite modern appearance, partly due to their larger destination boxes. As it turned out these were the last bodies to be ordered from this builder. The next four buses were double-deckers, numbered 59 to 62, which continued with the policy of having Daimler COG5 chassis with M.C.C.W. metal-framed 56-seat bodies. No. 63 had the same chassis as these but was bodied by Weymann's and had been a demonstrator for several months. It originally ran in a non-standard colour scheme and for many years carried a non-standard destination box layout.

The decision to replace the Birmingham Corporation tram service with West Bromwich buses led to further experimental buses being acquired so that technical information could be obtained as to their performances before ordering the buses for the forthcoming joint tramway replacement services. With No. 63 already in stock, the next experimental vehicle to be bought for evaluation was No. 64, which was a Daimler COG6. It was similar to the earlier Daimlers but it had a larger Gardner 6LW, 8.4 litre diesel engine coupled to the usual Wilson fluid-flywheel pre-selector gearbox. The 56-seat body was by Metro-Cammell.

The third test vehicle was a Leyland Titan TD5c with a Leyland metal-framed 54-seat highbridge body. Numbered 65, it had a Leyland 8.6 litre, six-cylinder diesel engine which took the final drive through a Leyland designed torque convertor to the back axle. The final test bus, again a double-decker, was numbered 70. It was an A.E.C. Regent, which had an A.E.C. six cylinder, 7.7 litre diesel engine, coupled to a fluid flywheel and a pre-selector gearbox and unusually for the West Midlands area, a Charles Roe teak-framed body with 56 seats. It entered service on New Years Day 1938.

In between all the excitement of the double-decker trials came four more single-deck Dennis Lancets, which were numbered 66-69. These were the Mark II model which had a more modern looking front end than the previous Lancets and had the usual clutch and gearbox, which was still the Department's choice for single-deckers. Externally the batch was identical with Jensen 39-seat front entrance bodies, but under the skin the last one was a very different vehicle. While the first three had the usual Dennis petrol engines, 69 had a four-cylinder diesel engine. The three petrol buses were quite lively performers, but the diesel one was quite noisy compared to the Gardner engines in the contemporary double-deckers.

By about April 1938, the experimental buses had been evaluated and it was decided by the Transport Committee to order 31 Daimler COG6 chassis with M.C.C.W. 56-seat metal framed bodies to the same general design as those being ordered by Edinburgh Corporation. The buses had Gardner six-cylinder engines and Wilson pre-selector gearboxes with fluid flywheels. The buses were of the same general mechanical layout as the experimental No. 64 and were numbered 71-101. 71 came into service on 1st March 1939 and the remainder with the tramway conversion on 2nd April. They were a wise choice as they gave trouble free service for many years, especially during the Second World War when their rugged construction enabled them to keep working with a minimum of maintenance.

In May 1939 another four double-deck buses were ordered, which appeared ten months later as numbers 102 to 105. These were identical to the previous Daimler COG6s. They were followed by two single-deck Daimler COG5/40s with Jensen 38-seat front entrance bodies. They were numbered 106 and 107 and were the last pre-war style of buses to be delivered as the war virtually ended the production of buses for a few years while all the country's industrial production was turned over to the manufacture of essential military equipment.

On the outbreak of war we were decreed by the Council to convert some of the old single-deckers to ambulances and eleven buses in all, including 57 and 58, the two 1936 Dennis Lancet's were fitted with stretchers. Other old withdrawn buses were initially kept, so that they might be cannibalized for their spare parts so that similar vehicles could be kept going.

By the end of 1942, many provincial areas were in dire need of extra buses. In London, because of the evacuation programme, the effects of the air raids and the Government's policy of moving war production factories away from the Capital, the need for buses in the London area was somewhat reduced. London Transport was therefore able to lend out fairly elderly double-deckers to areas of the country which needed them. With so much heavy industry and therefore many extra passengers being carried on essential wartime employment to and from munitions factories West Bromwich qualified for assistance. London Transport loaned three open-staircase A.E.C. Regent double-deckers; these were ST 554, 562 and 787. They retained their London Transport livery of red and white and I remember that they always seemed to work on the old Spon Croft to Oldbury route as well as the Stone Cross service.

Until 1943 it had been impossible to purchase new buses and although the double-deck fleet was in the main fairly new, it was getting a little depleted by the demands being made upon it. The Government now allowed certain manufacturers to build new buses. The Transport Department obtained in March 1943 the first of three double-deckers. Built to a standard Ministry of War Transport design they were immediately nicknamed "Utilities" as they were very spartan and lacked any sort of luxury or frills. Numbered 108-110, they were Daimler CWG5's. Like the tramway replacement buses they were fitted with Gardner oil engines, only this time of the smaller five-cylinder variety. They did have the luxury of pre-selector gearboxes and easy gearchange fluid flywheels. The Duple bodies were very much more basic. They were painted in all-over grey, had just one destination box and no rear window on the upper deck. Their final lack of luxury was that they had bench-type wooden slatted seats and backs. Despite this, they were a very welcome addition to the fleet. Unfortunately, just one week after the last of these buses entered service, No. 84 was burnt out at Dudley Port after an electrical fault so that we were only two buses better off.

Two second-hand single-deckers were acquired in the summer of 1943. These were originally owned by Southdown and Pearson's of Walsall respectively, but had been commandeered by the War Department before being released through the Ministry of Supply. Originally delivered in grey livery, these two Leyland Tiger TS7s were numbered 111 which had a Harrington body and 112 with a Burlingham body. Although welcome additions to the fleet, they were

81

not really suitable for stage carriage work as they had very steep steps into the saloon. These would have been bad enough but to negotiate them in the blackout was particularly difficult. They also had high-backed coach seats and narrow, deep-well gangways. Nevertheless they did carry passengers as at this time of the war any vehicle was welcome. They were usually to be found working at peak hours on the Stone Cross routes.

As the war went by further "Utilities" arrived in small batches. They were all Daimlers again but of the CWA6 type with A.E.C. 7.7 litre six-cylinder diesel engines. Numbers 113 to 119 were grey-painted Duple bodied double-deckers. Before the next "Utilities" came, three former Wolverhampton Corporation single-deck, rear-entrance Daimler COG5's were bought. I do not know the reason for their purchase, but they must have been unwanted in Wolverhampton. They were painted in grey before entering service and were numbered 129 to 131.

Between December 1944 and March 1945 two batches of further Daimler CWA6 "Utilities" came. 120 to 124 had Brush bodies and were delivered in the full fleet colours which, even if the cream part was a bit on the yellow side, was a most welcome return to normal. Buses 125 to 128 had Duple bodies but these came painted in all-over battleship grey. All of these had the usual seating capacity of fifty-six but much to the relief of the passengers they had upholstered seats. One very important improvement had been made on these wartime deliveries; all of them were fitted with 24-volt electrical systems instead of the pre-war 12-volt standard. A diesel engine, with its compression ignition, has to have a good speed of engine turnover to start it from cold, especially when the engine oil has gone cold and thick! In very cold weather, it was quite the normal practice to let buses run all night rather than stop the engines and then have difficulty in restarting again in the morning. The old 12-volt system really struggled to start the buses in cold weather but with the new wartime deliveries it became far less of a problem.

After the end of the war orders for new buses were placed but it was to be a whole year before anything happened. Bus 84 received a new Metro-Cammell body to replace the body which had been burnt out in 1943. Perhaps more interestingly, when No. 132, a Daimler CWD6 chassis was delivered some twenty-one months before No.133, which had the following Daimler chassis number, it was fitted with the unique 1932 Dixon body from 42, which had been withdrawn in 1942. It can be seen from this that the delays in obtaining bodies were very long, a fact which resulted in some peculiar arrangements being made for the bodying of the post-war half-cab single-deckers.

At the beginning of 1948 the shortage of buses was becoming acute once again. Whilst orders had been placed, there seemed little prospect of any immediate delivery and with the ever increasing demands on the Transport Department's fleet of buses, there was no option other than to hire buses from local operators. Four vehicles were eventually hired. The most well known was a Leyland Titan TD7 with a lowbridge Northern Counties body, which had been built in the early days of the war. It had been allocated to Gliderways of Smethwick for use on their munitions contract to the Austin Motor Works at Longbridge in Birmingham and was used by us, I believe, on the main route from the Hawthorns through to Dudley. An old ex-Southdown Leyland Tiger TS1 and a utility Bedford OWB, both from Hill's of Old Meeting Street, West Bromwich were hired and these ran on the Tantany service. Another old coach hired from Swallow Coaches of Smethwick was used on the Great Bridge route.

Eventually, Daimler CWD6, No. 133, entered service at the end of 1948. It was the last of the wartime Daimler chassis but was bodied by M.C.C.W. to full post-war standards as part of the next batch of double-deckers. These were six Daimler CVD6's, numbered 134 to 139; their body design was very similar to the tramway replacement batch of 1939.

Two more Daimler CVD6 chassis were purchased and to save time were bodied by the Transport Department at Oak Lane with timber-framed 36-seat front-entrance bodywork. 140 entered service on 10th April 1948 and 141 on 1st July 1948. This was some five months before the buses which preceded them in the fleet numbering system. About this time the oldest bus in the fleet, No. 32, was withdrawn for the second time in its career. Yet again it would lead a charmed life, to reappear as the 1951 Festival of Britain float. The wooden-framed canvas body was designed by Mr G. Knight and it depicted scenes of the different types of tram and bus which had run through West Bromwich in the previous seventy-odd years.

New buses still continued to arrive at the end of 1948. The Transport Committee had decided to standardize upon the Daimler chassis, with its pre-selector gearbox and the Gardner 6LW, 8.6 litre diesel engine, coupled where possible with the metal-framed bodies of the Metro-Cammell Carriage and Wagon Company Limited of Saltley, Birmingham. First to appear were 142 to 151 which had yet another style of M.C.C.W. body.

The five single-deck Daimler CVG5s which had been on order since 1947 eventually appeared in March 1952 with lengthened chassis and 30 feet long M.C.C.W. 38-seat bodies. They had cutaway rear entrances in the Edinburgh Corporation style which were intended to cut out draughts and to lessen the chance of accidents. 152 to 156 were used mainly on the 252 service.

As new vehicles were being delivered, so the opportunity to get rid of a lot of the now unwanted older stock was taken. This eliminated all of the Dennis double-deckers, most of the early Daimler COG5s and nearly all of the pre-1936 single-deckers. These old buses were replaced by the last exposed-radiator buses to enter service with West Bromwich Corporation. They were some twenty Daimler CVG6's with metal-framed Weymann bodies and rather shallow windscreens that rather detracted from their otherwise splendid good looks. Numbered 157 to 176, their flared skirted bodies looked particularly handsome in the elaborate Corporation livery.

In August 1952 a Daimler Freeline standee single-decker was tried out, but was as unpopular in West Bromwich as it was to prove to be when tried on the 28 route in Birmingham.

The bodies on some of the wartime Daimlers were in pretty poor condition and during 1953, 116, 117, 119, 122, 123, 126, 127 and 132 were sent to W.Alexander and Son, the Stirling based bodybuilder to be fitted with new bodies. The Leyland body off 65 was fitted to Daimler 125 and other early wartime Daimlers were fitted with either prewar M.C.W. bodies or better condition "Utility" bodies.

Early in 1955, Nos 177 to 186 came into the fleet. They were again Daimler CVG6's but had radiators concealed behind their "new-look" fronts and had Metro-Cammell lightweight "Orion" fifty-eight seater bodies.

An unusual bus came on demonstration from Leylands in 1956. It was fitted with a Leyland body and although it had an exposed radiator, it looked rather like the Midland Red SHA-registered Leylands. The bus was NTF 9 and had an experimental pneumocyclic gearbox but no examples were bought despite the easy-change gearbox.

The policy of the Department was to keep the fleet at about 115 vehicles and with the gradual whittling away of the pre-war fleet, a constant stream of small batches of Daimler CVG6's were bought. Nearly all of these had metal framed Metro-Cammell bodies. From this point onward, the scrapping of older vehicles and the purchase of new ones every year meant that the whole fleet could be modernized. This was done by the policy of the Transport Committee buying new vehicles out of profit and not going into debt by borrowing money.

Twelve new buses entered service on New Years Day 1957. They were 187 to 198 and had 60-seat bodies by Willowbrook. They were followed in December by 199 to 210 which were also Daimler CVG6's and the first in the fleet to be fitted with air brakes; they were also unusual in having air-assisted gear change pedals. This batch carried M.C.C.W. bodies and this builder now became the standard double-decker body supplier to the Corporation until the end of its independent existence.

1958 was a good year for the Department as two of the latest buses were shown at the Earl's Court Commercial Motor Show. Each of the buses was the first member of a new type. 211 was a light-weight underfloor-engined Leyland Tiger Cub and was on the Mulliners exhibition stand. 211 was one of three similar vehicles and these were the first buses in the fleet to be fitted with doors. The other exhibit, on the Metro-Cammell stand, was 214, a Daimler CVG6/30. This was the first thirty feet long by eight feet wide double-decker in the fleet and was the first of a batch of six identical buses. These buses were the first "New look" front ones to have the redesigned so-called Manchester style of bonnet which was to be found on all future Daimler orders. The extra length of Nos 214 to 219 meant that these large buses could carry no less than 73 passengers. So successful were these buses that the usual December delivery of new buses in 1959 was another identical six CVG6/30's, which were numbered 220 to 225.

Half way through 1960 came another two Leyland Tiger Cubs, only this time with Roe 43-seat front entrance bodies. They were numbered 226 and 227 and I remember that they were only 7'6" wide so

85

that they could manoeuvre more easily on the single-decker routes around Oldbury and Smethwick.

The first reversed registration buses arrived in December 1960, these being 228 to 232, registered 228 to 232 DEA, which were again Daimler CVG6s but this time there was a reversion to twenty-seven footers, partly because of narrow roads in Walsall and in Great Bridge but also to make them operationally compatible with the Walsall Corporation's buses on the joint routes.

A surprising purchase in 1961 were two ex-London Transport Guy Vixen's from the GS class. They looked to have Ford lorry fronts but with their Eastern Coachworks twenty-six seat bodies they were used on extra services such as those to Stone Cross. They were also both employed on private hire jobs and staff transport work. 233 came in April 1961 while sister bus was used for over a year by the Corporation Health Department and only entered the bus fleet in March 1963 as 252.

By the end of 1961 it had become apparent that the existing destination blind arrangements had become inadequate and as a result the next batch of Daimler CVG6/30's, numbers 234 to 237, which incidentally had one extra seat downstairs making them 74-seaters, had the new twin blind indicators. A similar arrangement was to become the standard and the next buses, 238 to 244, were similarly fitted. In common with the Department's continual attempts to upgrade the specification, three of these buses, 239 to 241, were fitted with fluorescent saloon lighting. By the end of 1963, five more CVG6/30s had arrived in the form of 245 to 249, and with them two more Roe bodied Leyland Tiger Cubs numbered 250 and 251.

The first post-war vehicle was withdrawn in October 1962 and the now redoubtable No. 32 was used for the last time in Christmas week 1963 as an illuminated bus before being sold for preservation.

The Department's policy of purchasing front engined buses was still regarded as acceptable and in 1964 there was a reversion to the twenty-seven feet length Daimler CVG6, with M.C.C.W. 66-seat bodywork of the normal lightweight Orion style.

The final Daimler CVG6/30s with Metro-Cammell Orion 74-seat bodywork came in 1965 and were amongst the last thirty-foot long, front-engined Daimlers to enter service in this country. In March 1965, 565 CRW, an Alexander bodied Daimler Fleetline came on demonstration and it became apparent that this type of rear engined bus was going to be the next generation of West Bromwich bus!

When it was decided to extend the 252 service to Wednesbury it was necessary to order low height buses if the service was to continue with double-decks. The vehicles which were ordered were fourteen rear-engined Daimler Fleetline CRG6LX's, numbered 101 to 114. They were built with chassis built several inches lower than standard. They had semi-automatic gearboxes. They had M.C.W. bodies with both their upper and lower saloons built to a lower height which, when coupled with the low build of the chassis, made for a bus which was able to get beneath Aqueduct Bridge; their front entrances had double folding doors operated by the driver. The low height was not readily apparent unless one of them was standing next to a normal height bus. These buses were very popular on the new 252 route particularly with the comfort of having doors and the added bonus of saloon heaters. Unfortunately the first vehicle was destroyed by fire at Metro Cammell's works and a replacement chassis had to be bodied later. This accounts for the break in the registration marks as the earlier buses were registered KEA 102-114E while the replacement vehicle was NEA 101F. They were painted in a new all cream livery with light blue relief and had white plastic covered steering wheels as a reminder that this type of bus was able to be used on the 252 route.

Just before West Bromwich Corporation was taken over by West Midlands Passenger Transport Executive the last seven buses to be ordered arrived. These were Nos 115 to 121, and had the same Daimler Fleetline chassis as the previous batch. The main difference was that they had distinctive Eastern Coachworks bodies and a different seating layout.

The last vehicles ordered by West Bromwich were not delivered until the W.M.P.T.E. had taken over. These were thirty-three feet long Fleetlines, seating 80 in Northern Counties bodies and were numbered 4005 to 4012 in the PTE list.

BUS FLEET SUMMARY 1914-1969

Fleet Nos	Reg'n Nos	Chassis make	Body make	Body type	Into service	Withdrawn
	EA 300-303	Albion A12	W.J.Smith	B25F	1914	1914
		Chassis impressed by W.D.1914; bodies to Edisons, see next entry.				
	EA 300-303	Edison	W.J.Smith	B25R	1915	1919
		The Edisons had the 1914 bodies from the impressed Albions				
1-3	EA 303/1/0	Tilling-Stevens TS3	W.J.Smith	B25R	1919	1930-32
		1-3 had the 1914 bodies from the Edison chassis.				
4	EA 302	Tilling-Stevens TS3A	W.J.Smith	B25R	1921	1934
		4 had a 1914 body ex-Albion chassis.				
5	EA 999	Tilling-Stevens TS3	Roberts	B29F	1920	1930
6	EA 2370	Morris-Commercial	Dixon	B14F	1925	1930
7	EA 2430	Morris-Commercial	Morris-Commercial	B14F	1925	1931
8	EA 2490	Morris-Commercial	Dixon	B14F	1926	1933
9	EA 2525	Tilling-Stevens TS6	Dixon	B32F	1926	1934
10	EA 2844	Tilling-Stevens B10B	Dixon	B26F	1926	1937
11	EA 3200	Guy BB	Guy	B30F	1927	1937
12	EA 3334	Guy BB	Guy	B30F	1928	1942
13	NEVER USED					
14	EA 3535	Guy BB	Guy	B30F	1928	1933
15	EA 3700	Guy FBB	Guy	B32F	1928	1939
16	EA 3800	Guy FBB	Guy	B36F	1929	1944
17	EA 3808	Guy FC	Guy	B35F	1929	1934
		Body transferred to next 17 (EA 7575)				

Fleet	Reg.	Chassis	Body	Seating	New	Withdrawn
18-19	EA 3861-2	Guy FBB	Guy	B36F	1929	1934-42
20-24	EA 4071-4	Guy FBB	Guy	B36F	1929	1934-44
25-27	EA 4193-7	Guy ONDF	Guy	B20F	1929	1938-39
28-32	EA 4177-81	Dennis E	Dixon	B32F	1929	1945-48
		32 sold for preservation				
33-35	EA 4371-3	Dennis EV	W.J.Smith	B32F	1930	1943-45
36-38	EA 4622-4	Dennis HS	Massey	L22/28R	1930	1944-45
39-40	EA 4727-8	Dennis EV	W.J.Smith	B32F	1930	1948
6	EA 5022	Morris-Commercial	West Brom C.T.D.	B14F	1931	1934
41	PL 6455	Dennis Lance	Park Royal	L25/26R	1931	1943
		Ex-Dennis demonstrator, 1931.				
42	EA 5202	Dennis Lance	Dixon	H24/24R	1932	1942
		After withdrawal body transferred to 132				
43	EA 5469	Morris-Commercial	W.J.Smith	B20F	1932	1937
44	PJ 1576	Dennis Lance II	Park Royal	H26/24R	1933	1949
		Ex-Dennis demonstrator, new 1931				
45-46	EA 6300-1	Dennis Ace	W.D.Smith	B20F	1934	1941-50
47-48	EA 6302-3	Dennis Lancet	W.J.Smith	B38F	1934	1952
49-52	EA 6304-7	Dennis Lance II	M.C.C.W.	H28/26R	1934	1951-52
53	EA 6308	Daimler COG5	M.C.C.W.	H22/26R	1934.	1952
54	EA 6870	Daimler COG5	M.C.C.W.	H28/26R	1935	1950
17	EA 7575	Daimler COG5	Guy/W.B.C.T.D.	B32F	1936	1951
		Body ex previous 17, EA 3808				
55-56	EA 7661-2	Dennis Ace	W.D.Smith	B20F	1936	1951
57-58	EA 7663-4	Dennis Lancet	W.D.Smith	B37F	1936	1952
59-62	EA 7665-9	Daimler COG5	M.C.C.W.	H28/26R	1936	1952-55
63	EA 8590	Daimler COG5	Weymann	H30/26R	1937	1955

Fleet No.	Registration	Chassis	Body	Type	In	Out
64	EA 9001	Daimler COG6	M.C.C.W.	H30/26R	1937	1956
65	EA 9000	Leyland "Titan" TD5c	Leyland	H28/26R	1937	1954
		Body to 125, BEA 735.				
66-69	EA 9060-3	Dennis Lancet II	Jensen	B39F	1937-8	1953-58.
70	EA 9064	A.E.C. Regent	Roe	H31/25R	1938	1955
71-101	AEA 1-31	Daimler COG6.	M.C.C.W.	H30/26R.	1939	1956-63
		84 rebodied M.C.C.W. H30/26R 1946				
102-105	BEA 32-35	Daimler COG6	M.C.C.W.	H30/26R	1940	1957-8
106-107	BEA 36-37	Daimler COG5/40	Jensen	B38F	1940	1958-61
108-110	BEA 608-10	Daimler CWG5	Duple	H30/26R	1943	1961-63
		108-109, rebodied ex-61-62,1956-1957. 110, rebodied ex-114, 1960.				
111	DUF 167	Leyland Tiger TS7	Harrington	C32R	1937	1952
		Ex-Ministry of Supply 1943, originally Southdown 1167				
112	CDH 838	Leyland Tiger TS7	Burlingham	C35F	1936	1951
		Ex-Ministry of Supply 1943, originally Pearson, Walsall				
113-119	BEA 113-9	Daimler CWA6	Duple	H30/26R	1943-44	1959-68
		116-117/119 rebodied Alexander H30/26R 1953				
120-124	BEA 720-4	Daimler CWA6	Brush	H30/26R	1944-45	1960-68
		122-124 rebodied Alexander H30/26R 1953				
125-128	BEA 735-8	Daimler CWA6	Duple	H30/26R	1945	1961-68
		125 rebodied ex-65, 126-127 rebodied Alexander H30/26R, 1953.				
129-131	JW 8114-6	Daimler COG5	Park Royal	B34R	1936	1950-60
		Ex-Wolverhampton Corporation 314-316, 1944.				
132	CEA 732	Daimler CWD6	Dixon (ex bus 42)	H28/26R	1947	1964
		Rebodied Alexander H30/26R 1953.				
133	CEA 733	Daimler CWD6	M.C.C.W.	H30/26R	1948	1963
134-139	CEA 734-9	Daimler CVD6	M.C.C.W.	H30/26R	1948	1962-64

Fleet Nos.	Registration	Chassis	Body	Layout	In service	Withdrawn
140-141	CEA 740-1	Daimler CVD5	W.B.C.T.D.	B36F	1948	1962-65
142-151	DEA 142-51	Daimler CVG5	M.C.C.W.	H30/26R	1948-49	1964-67
152-156	FEA 152-6	Daimler CVG5	M.C.C.W.	B38R	1952	1965-67
		156 sold for preservation.				
157-176	GEA 157-76	Daimler CVG5	Weymann	H30/26R.	1952	1969-73
		174 sold for preservation.				
177-186	KEA 177-86	Daimler CVG5	M.C.C.W.	H32/26R	1955	1973-76
187-198	PEA 187-98	Daimler CVG5	Willowbrook	H34/26R	1957	1970-76
199-210	SEA 199-210	Daimler CVG6	M.C.C.W.	H37/26R	1957/8	1964-73
211-213	UEA 211-3	Leyland Tiger Cub	Mulliner	B39R	1958	1969
214-219	UEA 214-9	Daimler CVG5/30	M.C.C.W.	H41/32R	1958	1975-77
220-225	YEA 220-5	Daimler CVG5/30	M.C.C.W.	H41/32R	1959-60	1976-77
226-227	YEA 226-7	Leyland Tiger Cub	Roe	B43F	1960	1971-72
228-232	228-32 DEA	Daimler CVG5	M.C.C.W.	H37/29R	1960	1972-73
233	MXX 341	Guy Vixen	E.C.W	B26F	1953	1973
		Ex-London Transport GS41, 1961				
234-237	734-7 FEA	Daimler CVG5/30	M.C.C.W.	H41/33R	1961-62	1976-77
238-244	238-44 JEA	Daimler CVG5/30	M.C.C.W.	H41/33R	1962	1973-77
245-249	245-49 NEA	Daimler CVG5/30	M.C.C.W.	H41/33R	1963	1977
		248 sold for preservation.				
250-251	250-51 NEA	Leyland Tiger Cub	Roe	B43F	1963	1976-77
252	MXX 340	Guy Vixen	E.C.W.	B26F	1963	1973
		Ex Corporation Health Dept,1963, originally London Transport GS40.				
		Sold for preservation.				
253-258	253-58 TEA	Daimler CVG6	M.C.C.W.	H37/29R	1964	1976-77
259-265	CEA 259-65C	Daimler CVG5/30	M.C.C.W.	H41/33R	1965	1978

101	NEA 101F	Daimler Fleetline	M.C.W.	H42/31F	1967-8	1981-83
102-114	KEA 102-14E	Daimler Fleetline	M.C.W.	H42/31F	1967-68	1981-83
		101 sold for preservation.				
115-121	TEA 115-21G	Daimler Fleetline	E.C.W.	H45/28F	1969	1981

Explanation of Body Type Codes:

The numerals indicate the seating capacity. Double-deck seating is expressed as a fraction, e.g. 45/28 indicates 45 upper deck seats over 28 lower deck seats.

The letter before the seating indicates single-deck bus (B), high bridge double-deck (H) or low bridge double-deck (L).

The letter after the seating indicates the position of the entrance: rear (R) or front (F).